Sunshine in December

A Memoir

Val McCabe

A catalogue record for this book is available from the National Library of Australia

Copyright © 2019 Val McCabe

All rights reserved.

ISBN-13: 978-1-87-692224-5

Linellen Press
265 Boomerang Road
Oldbury, Western Australia
www.linellenpress.com.au

Dedication

This book is dedicated to our children, Julianne and Steven, our grandchildren Noah and Maya, and to future generations of our family. I also dedicate it to my sister Olwyn, who was thrust into the role of eldest child when I left home. Thank you for always being there for our family.

Contents

Sunshine in December - A Memoir i
Dedication iii
Contents v
Acknowledgments vii
Prologue 1
1 - The Journey Begins 3
2 - The Early Years 5
3 - Growing Up 12
4 - The Journey Continues 14
5 - Come Fly With Me 20
6 - Early Days 26
7 - We Gotta' Get Out of This Place 38
8 - Riots in Rangoon 47
9 - The American Way 53
10 - We Will Remember You 60
11 - All of a Sudden My Heart Sings 62
12 - Is It Love? 69
13 - I'm Backing Out 82
14 - A Wedding in India 92
15 - Voyage to the Future 102
16 - Love Hurts 109

17 - Decision Time	154
18 - Home at Last	160
19 - The Summer of Our Discontent	172
20 - On Our Way	178
21 - Starting Over	183
22 - Darkness and Light	189
23 - The Abyss	199
24 - A New Beginning	211
25 - Family Business	215
26 - Phoenix Rising	221
27 - Going Home	227
28 - You Light Up My Life	233
29 - Sweet and Sour	238
30 - Marry Me Mel	244
31 - Return to Sender	246
32 - A Family Reunion	250
33 - I Still Remember You	254
34 - Moving On	257
About the Author	260

Acknowledgments

Thank you to my husband Clive and children Julianne and Steven for their love and support and to The Society of Women Writers WA, especially Helen Iles whose workshop on Memoir Writing rekindled my desire to finish this story, which I started almost ten years ago.

Also, many thanks to members of the Book Editors' Club who each waded through 170 pages of my life to give me advice and encouragement.

Prologue

When I left the north-east of England to work in London, it never entered my head that I'd embarked on a journey that would result in spending most of my life in a country at the opposite end of the earth, miles away from my home and family.

So, where is home? Is it, as the saying goes, where the heart is? And can the heart be in more than one place? Is it with the family you've known all your life, the parents who loved and nurtured you, the siblings who shared your childhood? Or is it only with the partner with whom you have promised to spend the rest of your life?

Or is it a place? Does your heart remain in the country of your birth, 'the place that our feet may leave, but not our hearts.' (Oliver Wendell Holmes)

For those of us who leave our home shores, it's all of these things and, once having lived in another country, many never manage to find true happiness in either, trapped forever between the two, torn between the love of their new country and the pull of family, culture and values which are bred in us from birth. Our perception of home also changes depending on where we are and our emotional situation at the time. Does going home mean going back to the place of your childhood or is it the place you live now?

If home is where the heart is, then my heart is forever divided between the country of my birth and the country in which I've spent most of my life. John Ed Pearce wrote: "Home is a place that you grow up wanting to leave, and grow old wanting to get back to". That was certainly true of me for many years. As a young woman, I was eager to get away from home, to become independent, to discover those "faraway places with strange-sounding names". But, once my wanderlust was satisfied, it was replaced by the longing to be in places I knew, with people who knew me.

People move to other countries for different reasons, but they all have one thing in common. They are all a little homesick at times, be it for their families, their culture, their food or just the feeling of belonging. Many struggle to survive in a world of strangers they can't understand, while others just struggle to survive, without the family support network they have left behind. This is often the main obstruction to settling happily in a new country, and one of the basic needs described by psychologist, Abraham Maslow in the 1940s: the need to belong. In the absence of friends and family, many people become susceptible to loneliness, social anxiety, and clinical depression.

This happened to me, and it is a story which will be familiar to many migrants. I was lucky to be accepted unconditionally by my husband's family, and for that I will be forever grateful. But I still wrestled with depression. You can't just put your old life on a shelf and forget about it. In my head, I was alone in a country where no one really knew me, or where I came from. My personality changed and for a while I became a different person from the lively and outgoing young woman who left England in 1967. Would I have changed anyway, even in my own country? I will never know.

I love Australia, but there is still a longing to go back to where I came from, to where my life began. There will always be a place in my heart that yearns for England. For the tulips in the spring, the colours of the autumn leaves, the dark nights of winter, heralding the Christmas season and yes, even the unpredictable summer weather. But Australia is where we built our family. This is where our children grew up. This is their home. My experiences here have made me what I am today, what I became along the way and what helped me to cope and grow with the situation. But it was a long and sometimes painful journey.

1

The Journey Begins

Foreign Office, Whitehall, London, England, February 1967

Harold Wilson is Prime Minister, the Beatles reign supreme in the pop world, the mini-skirt has arrived and Twiggy is the model of the moment. London is revelling in the swinging sixties and hundreds of young people are protesting against nuclear weapons while thousands of soldiers are dying in Vietnam.

And I'm sitting at my desk, staring at the phone, pencil in hand to protect my newly-painted fingernails, ready to dial the familiar numbers. I'm so excited, I can hardly breathe. Shall I, shan't I, I argue with myself. They'll have to know soon, better sooner than later. I take a deep breath and slowly dial. Here goes.

"Hi, Mam. I'm going to Burma. Mam? Mam, are you there?"

I look around and see smiles on the faces of my work colleagues, as they visualise her response to my news. But the silence on the other end of the phone is speaking volumes about the shock I've just presented to my mother. There is no smile in Mam's voice when she finally responds.

"Yes, love. I'm a bit busy now. We'll talk about it when you come home."

As I replace the receiver, I can see her now, my cuddly, little Mam, a goodly handful was Dad's affectionate description of his wife. She's standing by the phone in the corner of the living room, next to the kitchen; one of those old, black, bulky phones with a dial. Dad's behind the bar, just a few steps away, his elbows resting on the counter, supporting his long, lean frame as he chats to the customers. My youngest sister, Carol, 12, will be at school and Olwyn, 17, at work in a children's nursery in Washington, County Durham. Mam is alone with her thoughts, wondering why her eldest daughter has deserted her and why she needs to fly halfway around the world when all Mam's friends' children are quite satisfied living close to their families.

Now I'm regretting my impulsive action. I should have waited until the weekend when I could have gone home and broken it to her gently. But, I'm so excited about the prospect of new horizons and adventures ahead of me, I couldn't wait to impart what for me, is thrilling news. Of course, they all knew I would be going somewhere overseas, just not so soon and not so far away.

Three months earlier, I was working as a secretary in Sunderland, County Durham and living in Boldon Golf Club where Dad was employed as Steward. Now I was off to Burma, a place I'd barely heard of until an hour ago, to work in the British Embassy, with a passport that described my occupation as HM Diplomatic Service.

It had all started with an article in a women's magazine about secretarial staff working in embassies overseas. "That's it, that's what I want to do." It was as if those words were lit up in front of me, one of those amazing moments when the stars seem to align to show you what you're meant to do with your life. I wanted to experience other countries, other cultures and this sounded like the perfect opportunity. I sent off an application and then everything happened so quickly. After two trips to London for interviews and typing tests, followed by a medical examination, interrogation of my three referees and covert investigations into my background in my hometown of Bishop Auckland, County Durham, I was finally accepted into Her Majesty's Diplomatic Service. It was a long way in both distance and society for Valerie Dowson, a young woman who grew up on a council estate in England's north-east.

2

The Early Years

Bishop Auckland, County Durham – April 1949-1955

You had to go through a passage to get to our house. It was back to back with the house on the front. There was one big room downstairs with a black-leaded fireplace that Mam used to clean to a lovely shine once a week. The kitchen was in a corner of the room but we had to get our water from a tap outside. I can still remember Mam carrying buckets of water into the house to do the washing. She did this in something that looked like a tin tub with a handle on the lid that she had to move backwards and forwards to move the clothes around inside. Sometimes she'd stand me on a chair to move the handle until I tired of this activity. It was play for me, but not for her. Then there was the wringer, a contraption not unlike an oversized pasta machine. Mam would pull the washing out of the washer and put everything through the machine while I turned the handle. That's when I was at home. It must have been exhausting for her doing this alone.

Hanging out was probably the easiest part of washing day. We had a long line running from one end of the yard to the other and I loved watching the sheets fly about in the wind. And sometimes got into trouble for wrapping them around me. But drying was not so easy in winter. Even in fine weather, it was so cold that everything was frozen stiff. As children, we thought this was funny, but not so funny when we had to put up with a clothes horse in front of the fire for days. This was two wooden frames connected by a couple of hinges, a bit like the modern clothes airers. We'd put a blanket over it and pretend it was a wigwam when Mam wasn't using it.

The toilet was outside as well, an earth closet at the other end of the backyard. Four families used this toilet, called the midden, which was just a large hole with a wooden lid. One night someone forgot to put the lid down. My six-year-old cousin Mary didn't see the problem in the dark and fell into the mix of sewage and household rubbish. She screamed blue murder and Mam had to get the tin bath out and boil water to clean her up.

Upstairs there were two bedrooms with distempered walls and gas lights with white mantles instead of bulbs. My little sister shared a bed with me in one room and Mam and Dad in the other. When our cousins, Anne and Mary, visited we had great fun sleeping on a mattress on the floor.

Olwyn was born about the same time as I started school. It was April and I was almost five years old. My birthday was at the end of May. On the first day, I went with some kids who lived across the street, to begin my eleven-year journey through the British school system.

St Anne's Church of England School in Bishop Auckland stood on the corner of Kingsway and South Church Road. It was a good twenty minutes' walk from our home in Bridge Street. A long trek for a five-year-old these days, but considered quite normal in 1949.

On that first day, I must have somehow found my way to Standard 1 classroom with the rest of the 5-year-olds. I don't remember how. But I do remember we were all seated at wooden desks attached to a bench seat. The desk had a lid which, curiosity aroused, I couldn't resist lifting but quickly dropped when a voice shouted "You, girl. What's your name?"

"Valerie," I replied.

"Well, Valerie because of you, everyone will sit with their hands on their heads for five minutes."

That should have taught me a lesson, but obviously did not, because my next memory is wandering to the back of the classroom to investigate the Wendy House, a structure similar to the cubby houses children have now. Unfortunately for me, there were no similarities in classroom discipline. I was quickly dragged to the front of the class and told to hold out my hand. The teacher then proceeded to whack me twice with a ruler on my outstretched palm, before pushing me back into my seat. Not a good beginning to my education, but definitely a lesson learned: good behaviour means less pain.

At dinnertime, I thought it was time to go home. So, I did: across two roads, through a tunnel, along a couple of side streets and across another road. How did I do that? I don't know, but I know that Mam was angry and sent me straight back to school, on my own. Tough love. We learned to be responsible for our actions very early in those days. By the time I got back, everyone was saying prayers before going home, and the teacher was not pleased.

Bridge Street was built on a very steep hill. Mam would sometimes put Olwyn in her pushchair and leave her with me to take for a walk. On a very steep hill. Sometimes I'd let other kids push her up and down while I played buttony with friends, a game where you had to flick a button into a circle and try to pick it up by licking your thumb and pressing on it. You could win buttons by picking up other kids' buttons as well. I was once conned into using a sixpence by a bigger girl. Of course, I didn't win and Mam was furious when I told her I'd lost the money she'd given me to buy some milk.

Looking back, I realise that my early life was shaped by the poverty of the post-war years, and the resulting deprivation. When I started school, Mam gave me money every Monday, wrapped up in a piece of newspaper. This was 'dinner money' and we all lined up to give it to the teacher for our school dinners. Except those who got 'free' dinners because they were 'poor'. I didn't know what that meant, but I saw other kids pointing and laughing at them so it must be something bad I thought. Then Dad was involved in a serious road accident and couldn't work for months. No work, no money and free dinners for me. Then I knew what 'poor' meant.

Dad was in hospital in Durham and Mam could only afford the bus fare to visit him once a week. Those were sad years for our small family, and even at such a young age, I was aware of how the lack of money affected my parents. Sometimes I had to return groceries to the shop, and once Mam broke down in tears because I'd bought 30 denier nylons from Marks and Spencer instead of 15 denier and was sent back to exchange them. I still hate returning goods. But through it all, there was always love in our house. We always knew we were loved.

We moved from Bridge Street to Durham Chare, next door to Nana Thompson, Mam's Mam, when I was about seven, I think. I remember being excited because we had running water in the house. But no bathroom. Mam still had to boil water and fill a tin bath in front of the fire. And we had to share an outside toilet with the inhabitants of two other houses, but at least it had a chain to flush.

Even though there was never any money to spare, we were always well turned out. Our clothes were always clean and tidy and every evening before bed Mam would put rags in our hair. This was a very painful exercise but the resulting ringlets were worth it. During my first year at Grammar School, I was chosen to model the school uniform for the following year's parents. I shyly paraded wearing a green and white checked dress and the bottle green school blazer with the school crest *non sibi sed aliis* – not for oneself but for others. My sister Olwyn had the same honour five years later. Mam's standards never wavered, even when she was working. She'd be ironing at midnight, socks, sheets, underwear. Anything that was washed was ironed. Her home had to be spotless and her girls neat and tidy. No good being poor and looking poor, she used to say.

For Olwyn and I, the countryside was our playground. In the

summer, we'd lie on our backs in the nearby fields, finding shapes in the clouds, making daisy chains, picking bluebells and blackberries or jamjar fishing in the river down the Batts.

One day in September 1954, Dad put us on a bus and told us to get off at Cockfield, about an hour's journey away. I was ten years old. Dad's brother, Uncle Harry, met us and we stayed with him and his wife, Auntie June, until Dad came for us. When we got home there she was, our baby sister. Her name was Carol and now there were three of us. We'd arrived at five-year intervals.

That same year, Olwyn and I were chosen to participate in a church concert organised by the school. We got to the church hall by bus and Mam was assured that one of the parents would drive us home. Didn't happen. So we walked to a bus stop. A man came up and told us there wouldn't be any buses because it was after 10 o'clock. What to do? He asked where our parents were, so we told him Mam was at home with our baby sister and Dad was working at the telephone exchange. The man walked us down the street to a phone box and dialled, asked for Sid Dowson and explained the problem. Then he waited with us until Dad came roaring up on his motorbike. Now that was a Christian. There were none at the church concert that night.

Bishop Auckland 1955-1960

I survived primary and junior schools without too many encounters with the cane or ruler and managed to pass the 11+ scholarship to gain a place at Bishop Auckland Girls' Grammar School.

Changing schools was probably the first really stressful experience of my young life. I liked most of my teachers but the Maths teacher, a very strict and sarcastic woman, seemed to think humiliation was a good way to get results. For me, it worked in reverse. I'd always been placed in the top five of my class, so to finish 20th at the end of my first term at grammar school didn't sit well with me. It sapped my confidence and school became a mountain I had to climb every day, the first step being the worst, as I started to invent reasons for not leaving the house. Mam's words as she tried to help me deal with my problem are still words I live by:

"Valerie, love, if it's bad today, it'll be worse if you put it off till tomorrow. You just have to be strong and push through it. It'll get better."

My Mam, who had left school at 14 years old and had little education, was blessed with a generous supply of common sense. And she was right. Things did get better. In my second year, my Maths marks improved dramatically, due I'm sure to a new teacher, Mr Wilkinson, who was strict but fair. I loved French lessons and what's more I seemed to be good at the language, so I decided I wanted to be a teacher. I wanted to teach languages and was advised to choose German as my second language.

Most students in my class came from families much better off financially than mine. Often parents had to turn down the offer of a place at grammar school for their children because of the costs involved. Another factor was that grammar school students left school at 16, a year older than those from other schools, so a year longer without a wage coming into the family. And there was always the underlying prejudice at the time, that higher education was wasted on women. Our job was to get married and have children. You didn't need an education for that.

During my first year at grammar school, I began to realise how different my life was to most of the girls in my peer group. Saturday mornings, with Mam baking pies in a butcher's shop, and Dad doing shifts at the telephone exchange, I was in charge of my sisters and the shopping. This didn't leave much time for getting together with other students at weekends, making it difficult to form lasting friendships.

Every Saturday morning, I would walk along Newgate Street to the Co-op with Carol in the pram and Olwyn holding on. I'd hand over my list and, as I was being served, another shop assistant would give my sisters a chocolate biscuit. They were obviously cuter than me! But the sweets I bought at Woolworths with the threepence pocket money Mam gave me when she got home, made up for that. I was a big girl now.

I didn't have many clothes and I must have been the only student in school who sometimes had to wear her uniform at the weekend. There wasn't enough money to buy extra clothes. This situation did nothing for my self-esteem and confidence but was just another problem I had to push through, and I did eventually find my 'tribe'.

I never got to be a teacher of languages. In the first few weeks of the sixth form, my 'tribe' and I were asked politely to leave as we were creating a distraction to other students. I can't remember the reason, but we were probably bored. That didn't bother me too much. I'd been told that I would need Latin to teach languages, not the German I'd been advised to take in Year 2, so the school's way of dealing with that problem was for me to start learning Latin with the lower classes. How they thought I would be able to learn five years of language lessons in one year, who knows? But I realised that there was no way Mam and Dad would be able to afford to keep me at university anyway. And I was really excited about starting work. I'd been helping out in a grocery shop on weekends since I was 14. Now I was 16 and ready for the next phase of my life.

3

Growing Up

England's Northeast - 1960-1966

In England in 1960, careers for women from my background were very limited: teaching, nursing, office work, factory or shop assistant being the main options available. I enrolled in an evening secretarial course at Bishop Auckland Technical College and started work in a factory office in West Auckland. We'd moved to a bigger house on Woodhouse Close Estate two years earlier so both places were close enough for me to walk to work and college.

Although I was happy with the people I worked with, it wasn't long before I began looking for something more challenging. I applied for a position as a typist in the same company without success: I didn't have enough experience. So, I took myself up to the executive floor, feeling more and more intimidated as I almost crept along the carpeted corridors, and knocked on the door of the Managing Director's secretary, a lady I'd glimpsed only once, and apparently one to be feared. She must have been very surprised to see this sixteen-year-old at her door, nervously explaining why I should be considered for a position more suited to my abilities. However, she was very understanding and within a week I was sent on a four-week training course in Middlesbrough, where I was instructed in the purpose and operation of a comptometer, a mechanical calculator, now superseded by electronic calculators and computers. Instead of typing I would be immersed in numbers. Not what I had hoped for, but a step forward.

I was ecstatic, someone had listened to me. I'd been promoted, but it didn't make me very popular with the rest of the staff. I was told in no uncertain terms that I hadn't gone through the proper channels and who did I think I was. Needless to say, my appointment to a new department was not as pleasant as I would have liked. I was the girl who had broken the rules, who had infiltrated the corridors of power. The girl who had not used the proper channels.

Although I was made to feel quite uncomfortable at times, I wasn't worried. I didn't want to be stuck in a factory office for the rest of my working days and, as soon as I had some paperwork to prove that I could type at 40 words per minute and write shorthand at 100 words per minute, I found a job in a solicitor's office. From there, I moved on to other more senior positions in factory offices on the Newton Aycliffe Trading Estate.

In 1965 my family moved to Sunderland where Dad was employed as Steward of Boldon Golf Club. I got a secretarial job pretty quickly and assisted in the bar most evenings. Olwyn and I helped Mam with the catering side of things on weekends, which didn't leave much time for a social life. My boyfriend and I broke up after a two-year relationship. I was twenty-two and I wanted to get away, to break free. I wanted to travel but not on my own. Looking back, I suppose I didn't just leave, I ran away.

So, here I was, a member of Her Majesty's Diplomatic Service. Who would have thought it? Certainly not the headmistress of Bishop Auckland Girls' Grammar School or those straight-laced people in the factory in West Auckland. No, fate had a very different future in store for me. One I could never have imagined.

4

The Journey Continues

London 1966

On Saturday evening, 3 December 1966, I stepped off the bus at Victoria Station, scared, but eager to begin my journey into the exciting world of London in the sixties. Savouring my new-found independence, I took a taxi to the hostel in Hyde Park Gate, Kensington, secured for me by my new employer, The Foreign Office. The warden, a seemingly appropriate title for the stern-looking middle-aged woman who opened the door, checked me in and waved in the direction of the stairs.

"Up two flights, Room 201. Breakfast from 7 to 8.30. Dinner 6 to 8.30. Here are your keys, one for your room and one for the front door. In by midnight. And no boys in rooms. Understand?"

No friendly smile to make me feel welcome. No guided tour of my new home.

So, struggling with a suitcase and two bags, I climbed the stairs to the room I'd be sharing with two other young women. Standing in the doorway, it was hard to suppress the laughter rising in my throat, but I managed to restrain myself until I was safely inside with the door closed. The scene before me was reminiscent of Goldilocks and the Three Bears: three beds, three chests of drawers and three single wardrobes. There was no sign of the other occupants; after all, it was Saturday night. But various personal items on and around two of the beds provided evidence of their existence.

A gas fire attached to a coin-fed meter brought back memories. I hadn't seen one of those since I was twelve before we moved to a house on a council estate.

Dropping my suitcase on what I assumed to be my bed, I began to unpack. I opened the wardrobe door and was a bit taken aback to see the image of a young woman of slim build with short, dark brown hair. She was about the same height as me. Of course, it was me. What was I thinking? But I'd never seen a full-length mirror outside of a dress shop. Then I heard it. Silence. Everything I'd done at home had been accompanied by the normal family sounds; parents and sisters talking, TV, radio. I couldn't remember doing anything without some kind of noise going on. It suddenly dawned on me what an enormous decision I'd made, and an overwhelming feeling of sadness engulfed me. What was I doing, here in London, miles away from everyone and everything I'd held close to me all my life? I'd only been here five minutes and I wanted to go home. I *really* wanted to go home. Home to my family, to my own bed in my own room. For the first time in my life, at 22 years old, I was completely alone. I got into bed and cried myself to sleep.

I was experiencing my first taste of homesickness. But it was nothing compared to what was in store for me in the future.

How weird it was to wake up in a strange bed, in an unfamiliar room, with two people I'd never met before in my life. And how lucky for me that I was sharing a room with two young women who quickly sensed my mood and lifted my spirits with their own stories of leaving home for the first time.

On Monday, with the help of one of my new-found friends, I made my way by bus and tube to Westminster, and from there to the location of my first assignment in Her Majesty's Diplomatic Service, an unremarkable building in the remarkable city of

Westminster. It was here, in a small classroom where I, along with other novice shorthand typists, learned about the procedures laid down for the formatting and distribution of the numerous documents we were likely to encounter when we were assigned to our duties in the hallowed halls of the Foreign Office.

I loved it all. My new colleagues, my teacher, my surroundings. I was in another world as I looked out of the window at Big Ben and the Houses of Parliament. I couldn't believe I was here, living in London and working in the Foreign Office, or would be very soon. To my mind, I was now in control of my life, making my own choices, steering my own course to my future. I was the captain of my own ship.

As part of our induction, we were made aware of the various ways foreign powers could trick us into giving away our country's secrets, blackmail being the most popular form of extracting information from naive and unsuspecting young ladies. Such circumstances were so far away from our experience, and lots of suppressed giggles accompanied this information. We watched films of Guy Burgess, Donald Maclean and Kim Philby, the British spies who had defected to Russia in the 50s and 60s. At the time, I thought how awful it must be to have to live in another country for the rest of your life, never to be able to return. It would be like serving a life sentence in jail, a thought I would remember in the not too distant future.

We spent two weeks in this small room, before being assigned to the shorthand pool in Whitehall, from where we were directed on a daily basis to other parts of the building. Having reached the heady world of personal secretary in Sunderland, it was quite a change to be in a pool with other shorthand-typists. The shorthand pool was the bottom rung of the ladder of written communication. We took the notes and typed them out on special forms in double spacing. We were the originators of the First Draft which was then despatched up the ladder until finally, it would arrive on the desk of the person it was intended for. Would it be recognisable to us? I doubt it.

My dreams of being another Miss Moneypenny quickly evaporated. The Foreign Office was nothing like I'd imagined. Maybe I'd watched too many James Bond movies. The noise of keys being struck on twenty manual typewriters was, at first, a constant distraction, but it soon became just background noise, and there were other things to worry about, like finding my way along the maze of corridors to the various departments in the enormous building that is Whitehall.

The building is constructed in a square surrounding a paved courtyard and I was in the part overlooking Downing Street. That was another exciting view, watching the comings and goings at No. 10 before Downing Street became a gated community. My plastic security pass would only get me into certain areas, and I was often turned back with new directions to an office where someone was waiting patiently (or not) for a shorthand typist to arrive.

On my first day, notebook in hand and two newly sharpened pencils, I arrived ten minutes late for my first assignment, very nervous and a little scared, having crept silently through carpeted corridors under the disapproving stares of countless important dignitaries, most of them long dead. Luckily for me, the young man I reported to recognised my anxiety, and his comments about his first day in the 'rabbit warren' put me at ease immediately.

Most of the people I took dictation from were quite pleasant, but I sometimes had difficulty understanding their accents and I'm sure they had difficulty understanding mine. Adjusting to the new vocabulary was also a challenge, especially when trying to write in shorthand. The word Afro-Asian comes to mind. One day, after returning to the pool from a dictation session, I was having difficulty transcribing a shorthand outline. I wandered around the room asking if anyone knew a word that sounded like *afreshen* because that was what my shorthand outline looked like. I was terrified that I might never be able to decipher the word. What would happen then? Would I have to go back and ask? I doubted that I would ever find the place again. Finally, the pool supervisor came up with Afro-Asian, a word I'd never heard of. I had such a lot to learn.

✯✯✯

Every day I entered the Foreign Office building from King Charles Street, walking up Clive Steps and passing the statue of Robert Clive, better known as Clive of India, a name which was to play a big part in my life.

Although I was busy during the day and had made friends at the hostel, I was feeling very lonely. Used to coming home to Mam asking about my day, to which I'd usually reply with a shrug and a mumbled "OK", now I had no one close enough to talk to and so much to talk about. I was learning that family members are really the only people who are interested in the minor details of your life. It's hard enough starting a new job, but new accommodation, new rules, new transport, it was all a bit much for a shy, young woman from a small town in the north-east of England.

But it was also exciting. Just getting to work each day was an adventure. First, I took a bus from Kensington to Victoria and then the tube, but, having just become familiar with the underground route to Westminster, I discovered that I could easily walk down Victoria Street, a cheaper and much more interesting journey, especially passing New Scotland Yard and Westminster Abbey every morning. Being in London somehow made me feel I was living in the world, as opposed to a small town. I still feel that way whenever I visit London.

At the weekends, I loved exploring. Wandering through quiet, cobbled side streets resembling scenes out of a Dickens' novel, turning a corner to find myself in a miniature garden or in front of a small church, from where I would emerge into parks which were alive with people, ducks, and squirrels, even in December. It simply amazed me that I could be steeped in history one minute and transported into a bustling metropolis or a Constable painting the next.

Then, suddenly, it was Christmas. I couldn't believe I'd been in London for only three weeks. I'd seen and done so much and couldn't wait to get home and tell everyone. All the thrill and excitement of my new experiences were bottled up inside me, just waiting to be released. I'd really missed having Mam to talk to. But I had to get there first. It seemed that everyone in London was going north for Christmas. Fortunately, I'd managed to reserve a seat for the six-hour journey on a packed train from Kings Cross to Newcastle.

Dad managed to get away from the Golf Club to meet me at Newcastle station and it was great to see my family again. But my home had already changed. Olwyn and Carol used to share a room but now Olwyn had my room, it wasn't mine anymore. Things were not the same. It was as if I'd gone for good. And I had. I just didn't know it yet. This was merely another emotional bump along the way to independence.

But there were good things too, as there always are when you are surrounded by loving family. My little sister, Carol, had made a banner with "Welcome Home Valerie" on it, and everyone was happy to sit and listen to tales of my London adventures. Of course, I'm sure I omitted the part where I cried myself to sleep.

All too soon, it was time to go. I had to return to London and again I was having second thoughts about my decision to leave home. But I had to stick to my plan. I wanted to travel and after all, I was only a six-hour train ride away. For now; it would be five years before we would be together again for Christmas.

5

Come Fly with Me

London, February 1967

Returning to work, I was delighted to be told I'd been transferred from the shorthand pool to the Personnel Department, a move which reignited my enthusiasm for overseas travel, the reason I was there in the first place. I was so excited. They couldn't have sent me to a more fitting department. This was the employment centre for overseas postings and this was where the world became real. It was so much more than a map on the wall, as I became increasingly aware of the vast number of overseas missions around the globe. For someone who had never been out of the country, it was a dream come true. To think that I could be living and working in one of those countries within the year was amazing, astonishing, there were no adjectives to describe how I was feeling at that time.

I couldn't wait to get to work each day and to wade through the never-ending correspondence from UK-based personnel in overseas missions. Each year they sent in a report about their posting and their preferences for the next one. It was my job to enter the information on a card index, long before computers came on the scene. I loved working with people who had spent time in so many different countries and reading the comments made by the young women working in cities all over the world. I would sit and imagine what it must be like to live in another country, especially a warm one. I wanted sunshine on my shoulders every day. I wanted to wander around unfamiliar streets; to listen to local people speaking an unfamiliar language in an unfamiliar environment.

I was certainly happy most of the time and when I was feeling a bit down, I'd get the train to Uxbridge and stay the weekend with Mam's sister and her husband. Aunt Agnes and Uncle George lived in Iver Heath, about an hour away from London. This was my home away from home where I was always welcomed with open arms.

However, I was finding it very difficult to live in London on the small wage I was earning. £11 a week was about half what I'd been earning in Sunderland and even after paying board to Mam, I'd still had enough left for my personal use. Now I had to pay for the hostel, tube fares, lunches and everything else I needed to survive. It seemed like every week I was on the phone to Dad asking for money. I was enjoying my job and the lifestyle. I loved the theatres where, with my new friends from the hostel and from work, I would sit in the gods because we couldn't afford anything else; the shops where we couldn't afford to buy anything at all, and the company of my room-mates. Yes, I was having a great time but I needed more money. I needed an overseas posting. If I didn't get one soon I would have to return to the North East. I'd only been in the department for a month and my colleagues assured me that I would need to be there for at least six months before I would even be considered. What to do? Well, nothing ventured, nothing gained. What's the worst that could happen, I asked myself. So, summoning up all my courage, I knocked on the door of the Head of Personnel.

"Come in," came the response. I put my head around the door and virtually crept into the office. I'd never spoken to my boss before and only seen her a couple of times, so I was a bit worried about how she would respond to this relatively new member of her staff demanding an overseas posting

"And in what part of this wonderful world are you prepared to call home for a couple of years?"

"Sunshine in December would be nice," I replied.

After all that worrying, she was very understanding when I explained my situation and a few weeks later, I was offered a choice of Reykjavik, Iceland; Rawalpindi, Pakistan; Addis Ababa, Ethiopa or Rangoon, Burma. Reykjavik was definitely not somewhere I wanted to spend two years of my life. I wanted sunshine and lots of it.

Remembering my homesickness when I first came to London, I chose Rangoon because it was the farthest away from England and very unlikely for me to be able to pop home for a weekend, however sad I was. My friends thought that was crazy thinking, but not to me. What was the point of taking an overseas posting if I spent all my money coming home whenever I got homesick?

So now, three months after arriving in London, I was planning to leave not only my home town but also my country and my family, to spend two years in Burma, 10,000 miles away. Very scary!

It was all so normal for my colleagues in the Personnel Department. They'd all done this before, many times. For me, everything was new and exciting: a passport which I'd never had before, the vaccinations and even the mandatory visits to the dentist to minimise the need for dental work when I was overseas. Apparently, Burma was not renowned for its medical facilities. My emergency appendectomy, three months before I left home, had now become a blessing rather than the nuisance it had appeared to be at the time.

I would be away for two years. I'd be in a warm country and I was dying to know what that was like. I'd never been out of England before. The information I received on Burma gave explanations about the dry and wet seasons and advised me to take a hairdryer because the humidity often made it difficult to dry hair. What's humidity? I asked myself. Dictionary definition: the amount of moisture in the atmosphere. I couldn't imagine what that was like.

I had four weeks to prepare myself for departure and there was a lot to be done. It was definitely a matter of leaving home. I had to supply all my own household effects. I didn't think I would be doing that until I got married. I was setting up my first home, not in England but in Burma.

I needed to buy china, cutlery, sheets, pillowcases, towels and clothes for a warm climate, as well as a trunk to send them all to Rangoon. Fortunately, I was given an interest-free loan, payments to be deducted from my monthly salary and a list of places which would supply and organise the household items.

Clothes were another matter altogether. Shopping for summer clothes in February in England in 1967 wasn't easy. It was almost impossible to find swimsuits, shorts and summer dresses in winter. Perhaps now with more people travelling overseas on holiday it's easier, but certainly not in 1967. One of my room-mates suggested I buy lots of material and I could have clothes made quite cheaply in Rangoon. Well, that was an unfamiliar concept, fancy having clothes made especially for me. Made to measure was for rich folks.

Something else to be done was a typing test. Although I had a certificate for typing at 50 words per minute, I had to pass the Civil Service test at 40 wpm. This wasn't just a speed test, it was a collection of documents which had to be typed at an average of 40 wpm over a period of one hour, on a manual typewriter. Three times I tried and three times I failed. I was devastated. I had to pass the test or I would forfeit the posting and be stuck in London until another suitable position was available. Twice a week, I'd get the tube to a building in High Holborn, do the test and then come back and wait for the results which were phoned through later in the day. It was a case of fourth time lucky. Ironically, during my first three months in Rangoon, I sat another Civil Service Typing test and passed at 60 wpm.

Yet another surprise awaited me. I received an invitation from my future boss. He would be arriving in Burma a couple of months after me and wanted to meet for lunch. I was so nervous, this was another first for me, having lunch with a diplomat. We met at a small Italian restaurant near Trafalgar Square and he was so friendly and funny. We got on really well. So now I'd have something to look forward to, I'd be the only person in the Embassy who had met the new Counsellor.

Finally, the big day arrived, the trunk was shipped, my suitcase was packed and I'd said goodbye to my colleagues in Personnel and in the shorthand pool. As I left the hostel, even the Warden managed to offer a smile and a handshake.

Everyone was happy for me, but I couldn't help feeling a little sad. One of my closest friends in the Foreign Office had just discovered she was pregnant. She was supposed to fly to Singapore in two weeks' time and she'd been so looking forward to it. We'd even talked about meeting up in Bangkok or Kuala Lumpur, like experienced travellers. But, she waved me off with a cheerful smile and a promise to write. We'd been friends for only three months, but we'd started our life in the Foreign Office together. We'd met before work every morning at Lyons Cafe where she'd introduced me to croissants and real coffee. We'd shared our hopes and dreams for the future. Now, here I was flying off on my adventure and she was left behind to face the prejudice that still existed towards unmarried mothers in England in 1967.

Looking back, I'm so proud of Mam. She'd never been in an airport before, let alone a plane and as well as the emotional stress of saying goodbye to her firstborn, she must have been very worried about me. She told me later that she'd watched the plane take off and thought she would never see me again. But, at the departure gate, she just hugged me and said goodbye and take care.

There would be many more arrivals and departures, many more hugs of delight and hugs of sadness. So far, my life had been pretty predictable. Now I was taking my first step to a new one and I was terrified and excited at the same time. This was my first time on a plane, first time away from my country. I was full of anticipation and looking forward to the future and whatever it might bring. I'd been in London for three months and I was used to being away from home, I'd got over my homesickness. Or so I thought.

6

Early Days

Rangoon, Burma, 1967

In 1967, flights to Burma stopped at Rome, Zurich, Addis Ababa, Bombay and, finally, Rangoon. It was a pretty uneventful journey for a seasoned traveller. But for me it was an incredible experience. Just knowing that I was actually in those countries was amazing. I remember sitting in Zurich airport, mesmerised by the view through the enormous glass walls Then, a few hours later, comparing that experience with the colourful stalls displaying beautiful fabrics and all manner of unfamiliar objects in the small building that was Addis Ababa airport. Wonderful!

Finally, Rangoon, the next phase in my quest for adventure. As I reached the exit door, I was hit with a gush of air hotter than anything I'd ever experienced. Did I miss the bit in the Information Pack about changing into hot weather clothes before exiting the aircraft? I must have been easy to spot as I stepped off the plane wearing stockings, a dress and a cardigan, to be greeted by the wife of one of the UK-based Embassy staff. After being escorted through Customs and Immigration, I followed her outside to where a Burmese man, wearing a wrap-around skirt, I later learned was a *longyi*, and a white shirt was waiting beside a black limousine. Very posh I thought. Settling into the back seat, I expected the open window to provide a cool breeze. No such luck. Who'd ever heard of a hot breeze?

Burma, now known as the Union of Myanmar, is the second largest country by geographical area in Southeast Asia, bordered by China, Laos, Thailand, Bangladesh, and India. Its capital was Rangoon, now known as Yangon, and it had been under military rule since 1962. When I arrived, that was all I knew about the country where I'd be spending the next two years of my life. And it was oh, so different from England.

As we drove out of the airport, I was fascinated by the unfamiliar landscape. Women with baskets on their heads walked slowly along the side of the dusty roads. Others sat by the roadside on their haunches, busily weaving bamboo baskets. And there were flowers, lots of them. Women carrying or wearing garlands around their necks, in their hair, and on their arms. There were very few cars, but as the road widened, the traffic appeared and we passed tiny vehicles which looked like three-wheeled motorbikes, covered with orange cabin-like structures, and buses so full, people were sitting on the roof and hanging off the sides. Definitely not like England.

Pulling into the driveway of Woodbridge House, a white, two-storey building in U Wisara Road, we were greeted by a little man in a longyi, accompanied by a heavily pregnant woman wearing a sari. After informing me that I would be picked up at 8 o'clock the following morning and driven to the Embassy, my guide and driver disappeared, and I was left to follow my suitcase, which was almost as big as the little man who was struggling to get it up the steps and into the building.

My new home was a two-bedroom ground-floor flat with a lounge/dining room and an ancient kitchen with a kerosene cooker. Fortunately, I wouldn't have to use it, as my accommodation came with a servant. The little man I had followed into the flat was John and he would be working for me. What did that mean, I wondered? What sort of work would he do? I was soon to discover.

It was a bit of a shock at first when John started unpacking my suitcase and depositing my undies into a chest of drawers in the master bedroom.

"No, no," I cried, "I'll do that.

But he insisted and after bringing me a tray of tea, complete with teapot, milk jug, sugar basin, and biscuits, he returned to the bedroom to complete the unpacking of my personal belongings. Who was the boss here, I wondered?

Fancy having servants. Another first for me. However, I found it difficult to use the word servant, and would always refer to them as John and his wife. I never did know her name. In fact, I very rarely saw her after that first day. I couldn't wait to tell my family. But, wait a minute. How was I going to tell my family? This was 1967. The information on Rangoon I'd been given in London informed me that phone calls were virtually impossible between Rangoon and anywhere else in the world. The only communication between me and home was by letter, *snail mail* as young people call it today. From Burma it was even slower. All correspondence was taken every two weeks to Bangkok, from where it was collected by the Queen's Messenger and transported to London, then posted to its final destination. So, news to and from home was very irregular. For my family, waiting to hear from me, no news had to be good news. If they heard nothing, then I had arrived safely. Even local communication from Woodbridge House was limited to one phone halfway up the stairs to the next floor.

So, here I was, alone in a strange flat, in a strange country with a strange, little man bringing me a tray of tea. What was I going to do for the rest of the day and night? It was only 2.30 pm. It wasn't as if I could wander down to the shops or go for a walk down the street. I had no music and there was no TV in Burma. I had only what I'd brought with me in my suitcase. My personal effects were on a ship somewhere between Southampton and Rangoon and I had no idea when they would arrive.

Looking through the cupboards, I found crockery and cutlery, the basic necessities supplied to new arrivals until their belongings arrived. I wandered into the kitchen but John was obviously sitting outside the back door because he materialised as soon as I entered. This was his domain apparently.

So, I decided to explore.

Stepping tentatively outside the front door, as if I was trespassing into someone else's private space, I walked to the front gate and surveyed my immediate surroundings. To my left, the street disappeared into the distance; to my right, the same. From across the road came the sound of voices accompanied by strange music. A wall of bushes obstructed my view and I'd just started to walk a little further up the road to investigate when another longyi-clad man came running after me, waving and shouting something I didn't understand. This was the gardener, or Mali, as I later learned, and he was pointing back to the house. I got the message. I shouldn't be outside. Fine, I was happy to oblige. I'd only been out of the flat for ten minutes, but my dress was sticking to my back and my hair was hanging limply over my face. I needed a wash and a change of clothes. By the time I'd showered and found something more climate-appropriate to wear, I heard a car door slam and shortly afterward a knock on the door.

"Hi, Valerie, isn't it? I'm Judith. I'm in the flat across from you. Thought you might like to come over later. I'm having a few friends round. Just let John know you won't be in for dinner. See you about seven?"

There were four flats in the building. Judith and I were on the ground floor. The Ambassador's Personal Assistant and the Embassy Consul lived in the flats above.

Judith's dinner party was my first introduction to the lifestyle of members of the Diplomatic community in Rangoon. Dinner parties, sometimes finishing so late that we went home, had a shower and went straight to work. But, I also learned that in this small community, whatever you did, someone would know about it very soon. Judith took me aside that first evening and warned me about wandering about on my own.

★★★

As arranged, a car arrived at the front door at 8 o'clock the following morning. I was a little bit nervous but full of anticipation. New job, new people, new surroundings. What lay ahead? I was replacing a young woman who had married an American GI, but she wouldn't be there to hand over. She and her husband were not allowed to work in their respective embassies. He was suspended from duty and she had to resign from her position as a member of Her Majesty's Diplomatic Service. They were due to leave the day after I arrived. I was on my own. I didn't know anyone. But I soon would.

The car stopped at the entrance to The British Embassy, 80 Strand Road, an imposing colonial building overlooking the Rangoon River. I was met by Pamela, the Ambassador's PA, escorted upstairs and given a tour of the offices, wondering why I had to have an Embassy car when all of us in the flats worked in the same building? We were just about to enter the Chancery, the hub of the Embassy, when I heard a familiar Geordie accent and almost collided with someone leaving.

"Sorry," he said. "Ah, you must be Valerie. You're from my part of the world. Welcome to Burma."

The owner of the voice. This was Bill, and he and his wife and daughter would play a major role in the next two years of my life.

Back in my office, I had time to survey my surroundings and read the material which had been left on my desk, providing information about Embassy procedures. In the days before computers, a typewriter was the main piece of equipment required by a typist. My office held a typewriter, a Gestetner stencil duplicator, a Dictaphone, and a shredder. I'd never seen a shredder before. Special instructions: at the end of the day or whenever I left the

Embassy, I had to take everything I'd been working on into the Chancery. That included audiotapes and carbon paper. All used carbon paper, audiotapes and typewriter ribbons had to be shredded. One thing I found particularly funny, especially coming from the North of England, was that it was quite cold in my office, because of the air-conditioning. As I would report to my family and friends back home, I often had to wander outside to get warm. Another strange concept.

I would be working for the Counsellor, the second most important person in the Embassy hierarchy. When the Ambassador was away, the Counsellor became the Chargé d'Affaires, the man in charge. While the Ambassador had a Personal Assistant, or PA as she was known around the Embassy, the Counsellor had a shorthand-typist, probably to distinguish me from the diplomats known as First, Second and Third Secretaries who inhabited various other sections of the building,

My first day in a new job in a new country went without a hitch. I had my own office next to that of my boss and I had no problem dealing with the secretarial duties assigned to me. Not too different from what I'd been doing in London. But it was very quiet. Where was everyone hiding?

My boss was leaving soon, as his posting had ended. But before he left there was a lot to be done, especially to get important mail ready for Bangkok and the Queen's Messenger. Queen's Messengers are diplomatic couriers employed by the Foreign Office to carry important documents around the world. Every two weeks Embassy officials would accompany our diplomatic bag of correspondence to Bangkok, where it would be collected by a Queen's Messenger and hand-delivered to its destination.

I didn't have a car so, as I was working quite late, my boss took me home each night in his chauffeur-driven Austin Princess. That was the highlight of my day. It was so luxurious! On his last night in Rangoon, he asked if I would like the remains of his liquor cupboard. Having been in Burma for only a month, I hadn't entertained much and my cupboards were still very bare of everything. So, I accepted, wondering how I was going to collect it and transport it to Woodbridge House. To my surprise, when I got home the next day, the cupboard was full. Well, one was, and it was duly named the liquor cupboard. An Embassy driver had delivered three boxes of spirits, liqueurs, and mixers. I was still not accustomed to having things done for me rather than by me. I can get used to this, I mused.

I hadn't known this boss for long but I'd enjoyed working with him. And now I was looking forward to renewing my acquaintance with his successor who had taken me to lunch in London.

✯✯✯

I quickly discovered that although it might be quiet in the British Embassy, there were lots of people in the rest of the diplomatic community who were dying to see a new face, and I was soon receiving invitations to dinner parties, brunches or just for drinks. A major problem was getting there. I'd been in Rangoon for a couple of weeks when I was asked when my car was arriving. Now that was news to me. I didn't know I needed a car, but apparently, the Embassy car was only available to me for a few more weeks. I couldn't even drive. I had a provisional licence but had only had a couple of lessons when I was twenty. That was two and a half years ago. This was going to be another interesting experience.

With the help of Bill, my Geordie friend, some car brochures and another interest-free loan from the Foreign Office, I bought a Lagoon Blue Ford Anglia, or LBA as it became known. It was free of purchase tax too, so cost under £1,000. Incredible to think of that now. I submitted my provisional licence to the Burmese Licensing Authority and they decided that was good enough to provide me with a full Burmese Driving Licence. Wonderful! Now

I just had to wait for the car and hope it turned up with all the important bits required for it to work. From stories I'd heard, it wasn't likely. In the meantime, I was granted extended use of Embassy transport.

Three months later, the shipping invoice arrived and someone from the Embassy went down to inspect the car. I was lucky, all that was missing was the ashtray, the battery, and the spark plugs. I knew what an ashtray was for and I knew the car needed a battery to start, but spark plugs, what did they do? By now I knew a few people in our little community so I rang my friend Bob at the American Embassy.

"Bob, what do spark plugs do in a car?"

"Don't know. What do they do?"

He thought it was a joke.

"Ha ha," I replied. "I can't drive my car until I get some. And a battery."

Apparently missing parts usually ended up on the black market and I guess that's where mine came from, because when the car was finally delivered to my door, it was as good as new, except for the ashtray. It had to be driven to Woodbridge House so someone had managed to acquire the other necessary parts from somewhere. We were well looked after in Rangoon which was just what I needed on my first venture away from home. There was always someone available to help.

But before delivery, we hit what could have been a major hurdle. The car was accompanied by an instruction booklet with a red cover. This rang alarm bells for the Burmese government in 1967, when Mao's Little Red Book was a symbol of China's Cultural Revolution, required to be read and carried by every Chinese citizen. So I had to go down to the docks with Bill to be interrogated by a couple of men in uniform. Given the current unrest between the Chinese and Burmese people, little red books were not popular in Burma at that time. Eventually, having decided I wasn't a follower of Mao Tse-Tung, they signed a release for the car.

Then the fun started. My first few weeks of driving in Rangoon were horrendous, more horrendous for others than for me I think. With so little driving experience, I'd regularly forget to put my headlights on or take my handbrake off. Thank heavens there wasn't much traffic in Rangoon. Parking was also a problem for an inexperienced driver. Trying to drive the car around the back of the flats and into or out of my garage soon became regular entertainment for the servants. On the first attempt, I scraped both sides of my beautiful new car and backed into the big monsoon ditch which surrounded the block of flats.

"John! John!" I screamed.

Though what this small, bony man was going to do on his own, I didn't know. But, there was always help around in this small community. The message must have carried quickly because very soon there were four or five small, bony longyi-clad men lifting the car from the ditch.

I managed to end up in this ditch a few more times and I'm sure all the servants and their families, and probably their friends as well, stood around in the morning waiting for madam (that was me) to shout "John!" before they could get on with the rest of their day. My arrival home was another social occasion for them. They would congregate outside the garages as soon as they heard the revving of an engine. Maybe it was my imagination, but I'm sure the crowd grew larger each day until I finally succeeded in manoeuvring my Lagoon Blue Anglia into its garage space without assistance. I had to buy my petrol at the Embassy pump where the Burmese attendant filled the tank and wrote down my name and number plate. At the end of the month, the cost of the petrol was deducted from my pay, which was deposited monthly into my local bank account. Food, cigarettes and other items bought through the British Embassy Commissary, were paid for the same way. Life was pretty easy, really. I didn't even have to go to the bank to draw my own money. Each month, I completed a withdrawal form from the bank for living expenses, and the money was handed to me shortly after by the Head of Chancery, in kyat, the local currency. However, if any of us didn't draw enough, we were asked to explain why – in case we were getting money from somewhere else. This had to be investigated for security reasons. Maybe we were selling secrets.

John and I didn't communicate much. His English was limited to yes and no and a few other words necessary to carry out his duties. He cooked meals, cleaned the flat, washed and ironed my clothes. Actually, I think his wife must have done the ironing, but I rarely saw her. It was amazing. I'd come home for lunch, a shower and a change of clothes. The clothes I'd discarded would be washed and ironed and in the wardrobe when I returned in the afternoon.

Shopping for staples was done in the Commissary and each month I'd give John money for the meat and vegetables. His wage was 20 kyat a month. At that time the exchange rate was 13 kyat to one pound sterling. Not even £2 a month. Incredible!

One evening I arrived home after dinner at a friend's place and was immediately confronted by John shouting and waving a bottle of brandy in front of me. Alcohol and cigarettes were duty-free at the Commissary so I had added a few bottles of spirit to my liquor cupboard. He managed the words 'wife' and 'baby' which I translated into "My wife's having the baby, can I give her this brandy." Wow. That was fine with me. Having a baby without any medication sounded very painful. I was unsure about whether I should go and see if she was OK, but the cries coming from the servants' quarters behind the house brought the other occupants of Woodbridge House onto the scene and I was advised to stay away, the wives of the other servants would help. This was quite normal for them. Next morning John greeted me at breakfast with an empty bottle, a big smile, and 'boy.' He was the proud father of a son and I wondered who had drunk most of the brandy.

Apart from his duties as chief cook and bottle washer, John also had to deal with my reaction to the various non-human inhabitants of my flat. The tiny lizards which wandered around my walls and ceilings, I could handle, but reptiles in the bathroom. No way! I'd just started to run a bath one evening when a brown snake slithered out from under the tub.

"John! John!" I went screaming to the back door. "Snake! Snake!"

He walked calmly into the bathroom while I sat in the lounge, pretending to look at a magazine. I don't know how he removed it, but he did. I crept cautiously into the bathroom and looked under the tub to see if there was anything else there that shouldn't be. Then I realised how the snake had got in. There was an opening in the wall around the pipe from the bath to the outside drain which hadn't been cemented in. That probably accounted for the frog that puffed up its chest when I discovered it in there a couple of weeks later. Or was it a toad? Another job for John. So, after a number of emotional requests to whoever would listen in the Embassy, the hole was finally cemented in.

I was also a victim of mosquitoes. I would wake up some nights with bites which had swollen to the size of golf balls, sometimes twenty or more. We were lucky enough to have doctors who were in Rangoon with the Colombo Plan, a scheme developed by Commonwealth countries, to supply aid to developing countries in South and Southeast Asia. My allergy was soon diagnosed and antihistamine injections prescribed. There was also a nurse available at the Embassy who was able to administer the injections when the bites became really swollen and painful. And John was given strict instructions to spray my bedroom every night with a DDT mixture from something that looked like a bicycle pump with a canister on the end.

John was from India and probably Hindu. He never killed anything. I'd see a cockroach on the floor and he would slide a piece of paper under it and take it outside. Burma was rife with cockroaches. I'd never seen one before I arrived in Rangoon, but they were everywhere, especially in bathrooms and kitchens. Sometimes, if I got up through the night for a glass of water, a side effect of the enormous amounts of alcohol we used to drink, I'd turn on the lights in the lounge and hear a scuttling from the kitchen. Cockroaches going back to their hidey holes. I once stood on one in my bare feet, not a nice experience, so always made sure I had something on my feet before entering their domain.

On the subject of insects, one night I came home to find the wall above my bed covered with them. Not crawling around, but swarming like bees. All I could see was one big, black moving mass covering half the wall. I rushed to the next-door flat and asked Judith to come and have a look. She was older and more experienced than I at coping with the insect life of Asian countries, but even she was a bit shocked.

"They're ants," she said. "Go get John."

So, once again it was John to the rescue. I spent the night in Judith's flat and next morning they were all gone. How? I don't know. Did he spray and then sweep them up? Did John's Hindu beliefs that humans can be reincarnated as animals apply to ants? If so how did he dispose of them? With his limited English, it was impossible to find out. I satisfied myself with a picture in my head of hundreds of ants following a pipe-playing John as he led them away from the flats and down the road to annoy someone else.

7

We Gotta' Get Out of This Place

Rangoon, Burma, 1967

At Induction in London, they didn't tell us about homesickness. Maybe they should have. But then again how do you prepare for it? It takes time to build relationships, to become part of a group, to be accepted and to learn to deal with rejection. An occasional phone call would have helped. We'd been told that telephone communication was limited, but I wasn't prepared for the lack of communication with the whole world outside of Rangoon.

The isolation was close to unbearable at times. In 1967 there were no computers, no email, no internet. I couldn't put on Facebook that I'd just done a wheelie around Sule Pagoda or had dinner at the Ambassador's residence with some well-known VIPs. I couldn't get on Skype and have a long conversation about what was going on in my life and "Hey, I really miss you all". Letters took so long to get anywhere. I didn't want to say I was sick or depressed because, by the time my family received the message, I'd probably be blooming with health and staying up all night, putting the world to rights and drinking a bottle of brandy.

So, no, they didn't discuss homesickness; however, they did give us advice about sex. It went something like this.

"Sex. Don't. If you must, keep it within the Embassy."

Fat chance of that. I was the youngest unattached female by about ten years in the whole of the English speaking diplomatic community, and there were no single men in the British Embassy anyway when I arrived, which is probably why the wives were so possessive of their husbands.

The pill was just becoming available and was a very controversial subject. Besides, I wouldn't have known where to get it. There was still a lot of stigma attached to being an unmarried mother and what would happen if I became pregnant? I'd most certainly be sent home. I could do without those problems. The rumour was that it did happen sometimes and these girls were sent home for an 'appendectomy'. Well, I'd already had one of those so no cover-up there for me.

In Rangoon, I belonged to a group who were all away from home. In our quest for adventure, we were all suffering from nostalgia for the familiar and an urge to experience the foreign and the strange. That's why we were there and, as I was told by a number of seasoned diplomats in Rangoon, if you could make it there you could make it anywhere else they sent you. I think Frank Sinatra stole that line.

There were two songs that were invariably sung, either during, or at the end of an alcoholic evening. One was *We Gotta' Get Out of This Place* and the other *I Wanna' Go Home*. We always felt better, everyone singing together, British, Australian and American, all wanting to be somewhere else: Home. We belonged to a club of like-minded people and although we were often down, we were never out. We could always pick up the phone and mention one of these songs. Those were the code phrases, the cry for help. The call would go out and someone would be on your doorstep with a shoulder to cry on in no time at all. This was my new family.

One of the major problems in Rangoon was that there was nothing much to do. There were no restaurants as we know them, just small kiosk-style cafes which didn't look too sanitary, where people gathered, usually spilling out onto the footpath, chewing betel nut or smoking some foul-smelling tobacco substitute. We'd been told to steer clear of these places, and it wasn't as if we could go out for dinner or to a night club. We were all stuck with each other, the same faces at every gathering until someone's posting came to an end and another face arrived to take their place. We had to make our own fun and we certainly did that.

✯✯✯

Although most of us were homesick, that's not to say that we didn't have some good times. I have many good memories of my time in Rangoon. In fact, sometimes it seemed as if it was one long party, where work was incidental and our social activities were the main reason for being there.

But late nights and alcohol don't always have happy endings. One night, I arrived home in the early hours of the morning and sat talking and drinking. I loved these discussions. It was fascinating, listening to people who knew so much more about everything than I did. And I was enthralled as they recounted stories of their experiences in other parts of the world, some of which I didn't even know existed. Like Ulan Bator, the coldest capital city in the world. No sunshine in December there.

This particular evening, there was a group of us in Judith's flat. By the time everyone went home it was too late to sleep, so I went across to my flat, showered, dressed and went to work. I got through the day OK but was due at a dinner party the same evening, so when I got home I took a couple of aspirins and lay down for a while. I woke up at 10 pm! What to do now? Again, I was a little girl, as I ran across to Judith's flat to ask her advice.

"Send your hostess some flowers tomorrow," she suggested after a stern lecture on consideration and responsibility.

How? There were no flower shops that I knew of in Rangoon. Next day, I managed to get the phone number of a flower delivery business from a work colleague. So, I sent flowers. But I'd made a lot of people very angry. Apparently, they'd been so worried about me that two of the men from the dinner party had driven over to my flat and banged on the windows and door. How embarrassing! Later I thought: Well, why didn't they go and ask John? He would at least have been able to tell them where I was. But, would I have wanted two men and John banging down the bedroom door when I was lying on the bed in my birthday suit. I don't think so. I would never have lived that down.

To alleviate the boredom of endless dinner parties, two or three times a year there would be a special event put on by the British and Australian Embassy staff. One of these was an Old Time Music Hall. We dressed up in period costumes, the women in crinoline dresses and parasols and the men in 18th century-style suits, and sang old music hall songs, such as *Down at the old Bull and Bush* and *The Lambeth Walk*. My parents had good singing voices, especially Dad who, at one time, used to be paid to sing at some local pubs. However, this talent was not handed down to me and I was often told that I must have been in the back row when tune was given out. I mentioned this to one of my Embassy colleagues after the show.

"Yes, Twiggy, we know. You were standing right under the microphone for most of the time," was his reply.

Oh dear. I'd decided to just mime the words but my enthusiasm had obviously overtaken my resolve.

How did I get the name 'Twiggy'? Well, in 1967, Twiggy was a famous model who had a very slim figure and very short, blonde hair. I was a shorthand-typist with a very slim figure and very short dark hair. This was enough of a likeness for a couple of the American GIs to label me a Twiggy lookalike, so that became my nickname. Soon even the Ambassador referred to me as Twiggy. I protested so much, that one GI, Marlow, gave me a Shan bag, a colourful, woven tote, with the words "TWIGGY, SO THERE" written on it in huge letters. So, I was Twiggy or Twiggers or Twig and my flat became known as The Twiggery. As I said, there wasn't much to do in Rangoon.

I might not be good at singing but I was up to date with the latest dances. I never liked sitting down when I could be dancing. The Twist and The Shake were particularly popular when I left the UK, so I was asked to join the Australian Ambassador's PA, Mavis, and a young Burmese man to perform at a cabaret in a dance group called The Rubber-legged Trio, each of us dancing on our own for part of the act. Mavis and I had culottes made out of Thai silk; green for Mavis and orange for me, and the young man wore black. We danced to the music *Tequila*.

I was all abuzz when the cabaret finished and wanted to tell my family right there and then. Of course, that wasn't possible. So I wrote it all down in my weekly newsletter home.

Then Pat, Sue, and Daphne arrived in Rangoon. I hadn't realised that I was missing, not only family but people of my own age. Pat, a young Welsh woman in her thirties, with blonde, curly hair, was posted to Rangoon as a replacement for Pamela, the Ambassador's PA. She was the life and soul of any party and a joy to be around. Twenty-two-year-old Sue, an addition to the UK-based team, was an attractive brunette and just as lively, while Daphne, a replacement for Judith was about my age and from London. The daughter of a diplomat, she was a great source of advice and stories of places she'd been. Now I had someone in the same block of flats to talk to and we'd often get together for an after-dinner liqueur.

One evening, Pat came down to invite me upstairs for a brandy. No texting, we actually had to talk to each other in those days. Shortly after I sat down, an Embassy colleague arrived and soon it was two o'clock in the morning and there were eight people in the flat, all just passing and saw a light on. That's what used to happen in Rangoon, a quiet drink could turn into a party. Time for bed, I said to myself and made my way gingerly out of the flat and down the stairs. Once in my own flat, I raced to the bathroom and was violently ill. Then I slept.

"How's the headache?" It was Pat, the next morning, in my office.

"Mmm, don't have a headache. Why?"

"You should have. You drank a whole bottle of brandy last night."

"I can't have. I feel fine. A bit tired, but fine."

But Pat insisted that I had indeed drunk a whole bottle of brandy. She'd opened a new bottle when I went upstairs and Maung Maung, her servant, had just kept pouring all night.

"Well, I did feel a bit unsteady when I went down the stairs," I admitted. "And a bit queasy."

I was still not convinced that I could have drunk a whole bottle of brandy and not feel any adverse effects the next morning. But why would Pat lie to me? It certainly made me think about the amount of alcohol I was consuming. Must be bad when you don't even know how much you're drinking.

✯✯✯

The wives of UK-based staff often went home on leave for long periods of time, to get children settled into school or just to spend some time with them. I guess they were homesick too, but at least they had husbands, someone to talk to at the end of the day, yet their biggest complaint was being alone. I was at work all day and out most nights so I didn't really think about it, but yes, it must have been very lonely for them. As far as entertainment and shopping was concerned, Rangoon was certainly not Paris or New York or even Bishop Auckland.

Of everyone in our families, why is it always Mam that we want?

I longed to be able to call her, ask how she was coping, to tell her what I was doing. I missed my Dad and my sisters as well and also my friends, but it was Mam who always came into my mind when I was a bit down. I had friends in Burma but they were like me, friends in need of friends. There was no choice, we were all thrown together to work and play, waiting until we were released and sent home to await another posting or, in the case of some of the American military personnel, to return to the war zone in Vietnam.

This was Burma. I should imagine that New York or Paris would be different, better or maybe worse. Sometimes you can be lonely even in a big city. At least in Burma there were only two places to go: The Belfield Club, also known as The Brit Club, frequented by Australian and UK-based staff, or the American Club. The clubs were not exclusive to Embassy staff. There were doctors and other medical practitioners with the Colombo Plan and American Marines and GIs, many of whom had recently served in Vietnam. We could always pop into the Club for a drink or attend a curry lunch every Sunday. Saturdays we participated in events such as Fancy Dress evenings, Italian nights and the American Club often had Bingo going on.

And every country has its Special Day: America has Independence Day, Australia has Australia Day and Britain has the Queen's Birthday. On these occasions, we were all invited to an official cocktail party and usually ended up back at someone's house for more alcohol.

My first official British Embassy function took place a few weeks after I arrived in Rangoon. It was the Queen's Birthday Party and I was wearing a long evening dress for the first time in my life. How glamorous I felt in powder blue with long white gloves, but very, very nervous. At these official events, we were not allowed to speak to anyone from the Embassy. This was jokingly referred to as incest, so we had to mingle.

Not used to such sophisticated occasions, I wandered around

aimlessly, trying to look as though this was a normal event for me, until I was rescued by a gorgeous man wearing what looked like the uniform of a high-ranking military officer and with a fascinating foreign accent. Suddenly, Judith appeared beside me and I was quickly steered away. Apparently, Diplomatic missions overseas showed displeasure with each other by ignoring each other's presence at official functions. Why on earth invite someone to your party if you don't want to speak to them, I wondered. Talking to him was my first mistake as a representative of Her Majesty's Diplomatic Service. Maybe next time I'll ask who I'm allowed to speak to, I thought, or better still ask for photographs of those who should be ignored.

But, generally our social life was pretty much the same each week; invitations to dinner during the week, extended lunches at weekends or to more exclusive annual events like the Marine Ball. It was much easier attending the functions at other Embassies where I didn't have to be afraid of speaking to people.

As UK-based diplomatic staff, we were on call 24/7 and one of our duties was to be available to make up the female numbers for dinner parties at the Ambassador's Residence. Pat, Susan, Daphne and I took turns and, most of the time, we knew in advance if and when we would be required. Pat would do the seating arrangements and, if there was a single male, then we knew one of us would be attending. But, sometimes it was an emergency and we'd have to be ready and waiting for the car to take us to the Residence within thirty minutes.

My first Ambassadorial dinner party was quite nerve-racking. I was somewhat bewildered and in awe of the company in which I found myself, and making polite conversation with the other dinner guests was not as easy as it sounds. For one thing, talking about their jobs was not an option. So what else was there to choose from? After "How long have you been in Rangoon?" "How long are you staying?", and some comments on the weather in Burma and in their country, the conversation would be limited to the meal we were eating. Of course, there was also the problem of language. Occasionally I would receive the same reply to every question I asked: "Yes, yes."

As well as managing the discourse part of the evening, there were so many glasses, about eight pieces of cutlery and a small bowl of water to contend with. I decided to watch everyone else and follow their lead. The small bowl was a finger bowl and was used to clean your fingers after eating chicken. I didn't know that chicken on the bone should be eaten with fingers. My mother would have been very upset had we taken food in our hands to eat.

It was at one of these dinners involving a finger bowl that I witnessed a situation very diplomatically handled by our Ambassador. One of the guests, a diplomat from a neighbouring country, began to drink out of the finger bowl. His Excellency, always observant of his guests, lifted his own finger bowl to his mouth as if to drink and we all followed his lead. I don't know if he actually drank any. I didn't. We were always advised to boil the water in Burma before drinking it.

"Could we have some finger bowls now please?" he asked one of the bearers.

So all the finger bowls were replaced and the diplomat was saved from embarrassment.

Twice during my time in Rangoon, I was called away from a dinner party to attend an Embassy function. One of the dinner parties was my own and I had to leave my guests in my flat to make an appearance at a farewell gathering for Sir Bernard Fergusson who had just 'popped in' on his way from New Zealand where he was Governor-General from 1962 to 1967.

One of the advantages of having servants was being able to leave your guests, confident that they would still be fed. I would return to a flat full of happy people, most of whom probably hadn't even missed me. But thank goodness it didn't happen too often.

8

Riots in Rangoon

Rangoon, Burma, 1967

When I arrived in 1967, Burma, once the biggest rice exporter in the world, had run out of rice and many of its people were starving. According to the newspapers, which were now nationalized and run by the army, farmers had refused to sell their crops to the government and Chinese traders were hoarding huge quantities of rice in their warehouses.

To make matters worse for the Burmese Government, thousands of Chinese students began making trouble in the newly nationalized Chinese Schools and by May of 1967, these students, influenced by the young Red Guards in China, started to forcefully take over their own schools. The government took advantage of this opportunity to turn the focus from the ever-worsening rice crisis. For days on end, the behavior of the Chinese students was front page news. Newspapers carried photos of them waving Chairman Mao's Little Red Books and inside pages were filled with tragic stories of Burmese teachers taken as hostages inside the besieged schools. The Cultural Revolution had reached Rangoon. The Burmese people and their government were not impressed.

"Twiggy, I need you to pack up your things and wait for me in the Chancery."

At three in the afternoon? Definitely not time to go home yet. Very strange. It was June 1967 and I'd been working in the Embassy for only three months, but I knew better than to ask what was going on. Her Majesty's Diplomatic Service gave out information on a need-to-know basis. If you didn't need to know then you didn't get to know. The Ambassador's PA always distributed information according to this rule, so I packed up all my things very carefully; leaving anything behind was a very serious breach of security. I locked my office door and made my way to the heart of the Embassy.

"Do you know what's happening, Bill?"

"Sorry, Twiggy," he replied as we entered the Chancery together. "We'll just have to wait and see."

That didn't necessarily mean he didn't know, just that he couldn't tell me.

But I didn't have to wait long. A Senior Attaché soon appeared to tell me that there were rumours of anti-Chinese demonstrations in town, and for my safety, I would be staying with Bill and his wife Liz until further notice. Similar arrangements had been made for the other single females. No one was allowed to be alone. Bill drove me first to my apartment to pack a bag for the next two or three days, and then on to his house in the Embassy compound.

During the drive to work next morning, the gravity of the situation became increasingly apparent. There was something seriously wrong. The streets were littered with smouldering remains of furniture and burnt-out vehicles. Overnight, barricades had sprung up at major intersections, where we were stopped by Burmese soldiers with machine guns.

This made for a very scary and frustrating journey to work and every time they opened the car doors and peered inside, I heard Bill say, "For God's sake, do we look Chinese?" But, there was nothing we could do about it, and the soldiers didn't understand us anyway, so we just made sure that we had our official British Embassy IDs ready for inspection.

Staying at someone else's house had its own problems. Bill's servants were not as vigilant about spraying insecticide as John was and they didn't know of my allergic reactions to mosquitos. One morning I woke up with one eye so swollen I couldn't open it. I counted three bites on that eye, one on the other, a couple on my forehead and one on each ear. I looked as if I'd been in a fight. Thank goodness it was a Sunday and I didn't have to go to work, but I definitely needed to see a doctor. Another job for Bill. He took me to an American doctor who was always happy to oblige with an out-of-hours consultation and an anti-histamine injection, even on a Sunday.

Then, to make things worse, my boss called. He needed me at the Embassy to prepare some urgent documents, ready for the Diplomatic bag the next day. I couldn't see out of one eye and the other was a lazy eye, so I couldn't see much out of that one either. It would take at least twenty-four hours for the swelling to subside, so I wasn't very popular with Pat who had to take my place.

We soon became accustomed to the stop-and-search tactics whenever we ventured outside, but, a few days later, things began to get personal and my heart sank as we drove past buildings usually occupied by local Chinese businesses.

"Oh no."

My voice echoed the horror we were all feeling. Hairdryers, sewing machines and other evidence of commercial activity were scattered along the side of the road, apparently flung through the smashed windows of these oh so familiar buildings.

"Do you think they're all right?"

I was referring to my young, female hairdresser and the very talented and patient tailor who managed to create beautiful outfits from my amateurish attempts at dress designing. Nobody replied. Where were our Chinese friends? And what would they do now without the tools of their trade? Sadly, we never found out. I asked my boss if it was possible to get some information about what had happened to them, but the look on his face asked me if I really wanted to know. Later that day we learned that a curfew had been imposed: it was now illegal to be on the streets between 6 pm and 6 am.

I was allowed to return home at the end of the first week of curfew, wondering how we would all relieve the boredom of our imposed confinement and how long it would last. But I'd underestimated the creativity of the American military staff, who had decided that if we couldn't go out then we'd have to stay in. Together. They organised curfew parties at the Marine House and GI homes around Rangoon. We arrived before 6 pm and left after 6 am, falling asleep anywhere we could find, never knowing who we would wake up next to. Of course this was a great source of silly conversation.

"Who did you sleep with last night?"

Or, even weeks later.

"Have you ever slept with …..?"

We secretaries were so protected from the outside world that, although we had seen evidence of anti-Chinese activity, we thought it was under control. One night I came face to face with the awful reality of what was really going on around us.

A US marine was driving some of us home from a lunch party. He'd only been in Rangoon for a couple of weeks so it wasn't surprising that he took a few wrong turns. We'd left the party at about 5 pm, which should have given us enough time to get home, but it was past six when we were stopped and surrounded by Burmese soldiers. Guns were pointed at us as we were ordered out of the car and shouted at in Burmese. With trembling hands, I managed to find my Embassy ID and eventually we were allowed to get back in the car and continue on our way, but not before witnessing passengers from a car in front of us being beaten and dragged into a military vehicle.

Our driver was on R&R from Vietnam and the sound of the bolt being pulled back on one of the guns shook him up so much that one of us had to take over and drive back to the Marine House, where we remained for the rest of the night. My ID was returned to the Embassy the next day and I was reprimanded for breaching the military curfew, showing disrespect for the rules of the host country. Not an experience I would ever want to repeat, and a reminder that, beneath its quiet and orderly facade, Burma was under military rule, a government which was not afraid to use force and intimidation to suppress any anti-government behaviour.

The curfew lasted for six weeks, and everything returned to normal. For us. We still didn't know that during that time, while we were continuing with our daily lives and having fun at our parties, students were being burnt alive in their schools and Chinese people were dying on the streets of Rangoon. I had thought that the burning of their tools of trade was the worst that had happened to the Chinese people. But no. Out-of-control mobs had entered China Town, looting and burning shops and houses and slaughtering their occupants. Some were thrown alive from the second and third floors of buildings while others, including women, jumped with their children to avoid being tortured. And we were not alone in our ignorance of the atrocities being carried out in Burma. A British businessman, stranded in Rangoon during the riots, offered to take letters home for us, to let our parents know that we were safe and well and the riots were over. Responses arrived a few weeks later. What riots?

Chairman Mao's Cultural Revolution was at its height in 1967 and, just as our families were unaware of what was happening in Burma, we were unaware of the atrocities happening to members of foreign embassies in China, including our own diplomats in Peking. Phone lines were cut and with them, all lines to London, as Red Guards set fire to the British Embassy, and our colleagues retreated to the Embassy's secure area, finally emerging to be seized by chanting Red Guards. They finally reached safety when the People's Liberation Army intervened and got them to the Albanian Embassy, from where they could see their own Embassy ablaze. And The Foreign Office had no way of knowing what was happening to their people in Peking.

9

The American Way

Rangoon, Burma, 1967-1968

Most of our leisure time in Burma was spent in the company of Americans. GIs and Marines were the only unattached young men in Rangoon we ever met, and there weren't many young females, so we naturally drifted towards one another. I think the Americans must have got a bit tired of their men being caught by foreign women. I replaced a girl who married a GI and during my posting, the Australian Ambassador's PA married another.

Although I'd had a couple of boyfriends in England, I'd never had friends who were boys. This was a new and enlightening experience. It was so good to be able to talk to a member of the opposite sex without the added complication of an emotional attachment, although it took a while for me to feel comfortable with friendly hugs.

The Marines shared the Marine House in Burma and most of the GIs lived in groups, three or four of them together. I got along really well with one of the GIs. His name was Bob and we became good friends, but his housemates didn't share his enthusiasm for my company and didn't hesitate to show it.

They'd just finished dinner one evening when I called around in my Lagoon Blue Anglia. The other three had Burmese girlfriends who lived there most of the time and none of them were happy to see me. I'd never been an adventurous eater, especially since my first

Chinese meal left me with a shellfish intolerance. However, I'd quickly acquired a taste for curry at the Brit Club, which proved to be quite advantageous for me this evening. One of the GIs asked if I'd like to try a little of the curry they'd just had for dinner. Having already eaten, I declined. "It's probably too hot for you anyway," said one. "Brit food is tasteless."

Well, that was a red rag to a bull. It was a typical remark from Americans to the British. There were often comments about the fall of the British Empire or the Boston Tea Party but they were mostly in fun. This was different. I knew they wanted to embarrass me. I responded as they knew I would, and accepted a plate of the supposedly hot curry. And, yes it was hot, very hot. I wanted to push it away, I wanted to cough, I was perspiring, but somehow I summoned up all my will power and cleaned the plate. Admiration shone from their faces and we were good friends for the rest of my time in Rangoon. They were always ready to come to my assistance if and when required as I discovered a few weeks later.

At the American Club one evening, one of a group of visiting American navy officers kept pestering me.

"Well, let me take you home," he pleaded.

"No thanks, I have my own transport," I replied.

However, as I walked to my car, I heard voices raised and turned to see one of my new 'good friends' in an altercation with my pesterer. My friend had been aware of the problem during the evening so decided to keep an eye on the situation. He saw the officer follow me out of the club and gave him a piece of his mind. That made me feel very protected.

He wasn't always there to help though. And I was old enough to look after myself, I thought. After dinner at an American friend's house one evening I was given a lift home by one of the girls from the American Embassy who was taking some Air Force officers back to their hotel. Saying goodnight, I got to my door and turned to find one of the officers behind me.

"Thought we could have a nightcap," he said.

"And how are you going to get home?"

"I'll get a taxi. We're leaving at 5.00 am. Just want to make the night last a bit longer."

After rejecting his amorous advances, I finally persuaded him to take no for an answer and call a taxi. This had to be done as quietly as possible from the only phone, located on the staircase. To our surprise, Burmese taxi drivers didn't seem to want to work at 11 pm. He tried calling the other officers without success. So what to do? There were only two options: he'd have to walk or sleep on the couch. As neither of us had any idea of how far away his accommodation was, or how to get there, the choice was already made for us, he'd have to sleep on the couch. Fortunately for me, there was a lock on my bedroom door, though he assured me he was an honourable man.

When I woke next morning, he was gone. But that wasn't the end of it. The Ambassador's PA must have heard us making phone calls or seen him leave in a taxi in the morning. She gave me a long lecture about having men stay the night and how it ruined the reputations of the British females. Oh dear! Now I was being portrayed as a promiscuous female. And it didn't take long for the news to get around the American Embassy that one of the Air Force officers had stayed the night at Twiggy's.

★★★

One evening, again at Bob's house, we heard a bit of a commotion outside. Car horns blaring and people yelling. Then the other three GIs came running through the lounge and out of the front door.

"What's happening?" I asked.

"Sounds like there's a commissary plane arriving," Bob replied. "Do you want to go along with them?"

"What's so fascinating about food arriving?"

"It's the bread. Come on, let's go."

The bread was the big attraction. The American supply planes always carried loaves of fresh white sliced bread on board, so we all drove out to the airstrip where the pilot and his team were unloading the supplies. That's how starved we were for the taste of Western-style bread. We picked up half a dozen loaves and no one spoke on the way back. We all had our mouths full and there were groans of pleasure as we rediscovered the delights of plain white slices of bread. What a treat!

That was the thing about Burma, little things meant a lot and could lift your spirits and keep you going for days.

I had many arguments with the Americans about our language differences. To some it was funny and we laughed together but others could get quite offended, and sometimes offensive.

I could never understand why crisps were called chips and chips were referred to as fries. There were other strange disparities between the meanings of certain phrases too. I'd insist I was correct because English was taken to America by the English, and they'd retaliate with: "Whatever happened to the British Empire?" But it was all in good fun. If I felt someone was getting upset, I would retire from the conversation. However, sometimes what was a casual, common phrase in England, would become an embarrassment for me, as happened one night at a party at the Marine House.

"Hey, Twigs," shouted one of the Marines. "We passed your house last night. We were going to pop in but the place was in darkness. You sick or something?"

To which I replied, "No, I went to bed early last night. You should have come and knocked me up."

Mmmm – silence, a few stares, followed by guffaws of laughter. Needless to say, I never said that again, and it was still haunting me months later. How was I to know that to knock someone up meant to get them pregnant in American speak? At home it meant to wake me up by knocking on the door.

I turned twenty-three a couple of months after arriving in Rangoon, so my new friends and colleagues decided this was worth a celebration at the Brit Club. During the evening, Bill – the Geordie – and a couple of the Embassy wives said they needed to take me home to see something. Home was about twenty minutes away so I was a bit confused and nervous, especially as they all came with me – Bill, Liz, Bridget, and Pamela. What had I done now?

When we got to Woodbridge House, Lee, a GI who'd arrived in Rangoon about the same time as I, met us there. We'd had dinner together a few times and I'd gone with him to look at some furniture for his room. What was going on? We followed Bill and Liz into the bedroom, where, in a corner, looking like it belonged there, was a teak dressing table I'd admired in the furniture store. Talk about surprise, shock was more like it. How had he managed to get it into my flat? Bill confessed that he'd taken my keys from my handbag and helped with the surprise. I didn't even know they'd left the party.

Mam had always told me never to accept gifts from men I didn't know well. I certainly didn't know Lee well enough to accept such a gift and wasn't sure what to do. A heavy, teak dressing table is a bit difficult to give back. However, my chaperones were there to advise me, they obviously knew I needed guidance. They said I could keep it or reject it. Lee had assured them it came without strings. It was just a thank you for helping him. So, I kept it.

Was it the Americans who introduced me to the pleasures and

perils of alcohol, or was it the lifestyle of the diplomatic community in general? A bit of both I guess. At home, my drinks had been limited to beer, Babycham and port and lemon. That was before I arrived in Burma where I soon discovered that if I asked for a glass of lemonade it usually came with vodka or gin. But, with the help of my friends at small dinner parties, I began to appreciate the differences and finally found my drink was scotch and soda, and a brandy after dinner.

Any social occasion involving Americans had to include the Slop, a sort of communal dance always done to the song *The Bloody Red Baron*. I still have to smile whenever I hear it on the radio. Someone would put the record on and a big WHOOP would go up and we'd all form lines trying to keep pace with the music.

But it wasn't all fun and games for these young men. One of the most traumatic situations I experienced in Burma, and which made all thoughts of home pale into insignificance, was the attack on the US Embassy in Saigon in January 1968. I was at the Marine House in Rangoon when the Sergeant got the news. It was so distressing to see these young men cry. Marines in Burma guarded their Embassy and the same applied to other US Missions, Saigon included. In the attack at least three Marines had been killed. All had been friends or colleagues of those sitting around me when they heard the news.

In November of my first year in Rangoon, I was invited to the Marine Ball. A very glamorous experience. My escort presented me with a corsage. He'd asked the colour of my dress and arranged for a corsage to complement my pale blue gown. I wore it on my wrist on top of my long white gloves and we were driven to the ball in a limousine. I felt like a movie star.

My American friends made life more fun, more interesting, and kept me sane throughout my time in Burma. I can thank them for introducing me to pizza, moussaka, pumpkin pie, and French fries; for the *Bloody Red Baron* and the Slop, which my husband and I still manage to perform whenever we hear that song; for lifting my spirits when I was down; for accepting me into their homes and allowing me to share their lives; for the crazy times, hurtling around Rangoon in my LBA during the early hours of the morning, dancing around University Apartments wringing wet during the Water Festival and generally bringing this shy young Brit out of her shell. Looking back, I have to say: Thank you, guys. I had a ball.

10

We Will Remember You

November 1967

After a very late night at the Marine Ball, tired and bleary-eyed, I joined the rest of the British Embassy staff early the next morning at the Armistice Day Ceremony at Taukkyan, the largest of the three war cemeteries in Burma.

The Cemetery was created in 1951 for the reception of graves from four other battlefield cemeteries and also contains The Rangoon Memorial, bearing the names of men of the Commonwealth land forces who died during the campaigns in Burma, and who have no known grave.

The Taukkyan Cremation Memorial, commemorating more than a thousand Second World War casualties, can also be seen at this Cemetery, together with another commemorating forty-five servicemen of both wars, who died and were buried elsewhere in Burma, but whose graves could not be maintained.

We were moved to tears as we spent an emotional couple of hours at the gravesides. This was the last resting place of soldiers as young as eighteen, who fought and died in this country, so far away from home. We stood in silence as we read the names of those with no known graves, but still remembered on a memorial for those 'Known only to God.' Yet these were men who were also known to mothers and fathers, sisters and brothers, friends and relatives, who have no grave to visit, no place to lay flowers, no place to stand awhile and remember; their memories kept alive through photographs and stories passed down to their children, grandchildren, nieces, and nephews. Every year on 11 November we pause to remember them, but here, in a place so far away from home, the true significance of the sacrifice these young men made really hits home.

Taukkyan

If I could look on this fair land
Through eyes of you now dead
What would I see I wonder
Would I look on it with dread?

Would I see the smiling faces
Of Burmese passing by
Would the Shwedagon Pagoda
Mean the same to you as I?

Or would I see the face of death
Disguised in human form
The way you did oh valiant souls
The year that I was born.

'Twas four and twenty years ago
He called you from your toil
Who lived and fought for England
To die on Burma's soil

Htaukkyan was built for you brave hearts
Who never more will roam
That you might sleep your last long sleep
Six thousand miles from home.

Rangoon, November 1967

11

All of a Sudden My Heart Sings

There's only one place to be on New Year's Eve, where I'd always been: at home, surrounded by family and friends. It was my first New Year away from home and I definitely didn't feel like socialising. I'd become very close to Bill and Liz Dixon, but they'd finished their posting and were now in Bombay, India. I hadn't been in Rangoon a year yet and I didn't know how I was going to survive another. I did have a choice though. I could take home leave after one year and then return for another year, or I could stay for the full eighteen months and go home to wait for another posting. I was seriously thinking about the one-year option. At this stage, even three months seemed like an eternity. Although I realised how fortunate I was to have the opportunity to experience the life of the people and culture of this country, I was ready to go home. What good is all this if you can't share it with the people you love.

Little did I know that love was on the way.

✯✯✯

"Come on, Twiggy, you have to come. You can't sit here on your own, that's depressing."

The party was at one of the GI houses and I knew it would be good, but I really would rather have stayed home. I was just getting over a bout of the Rangoon trots, the name we used for an upset tummy, so that was my excuse to my friends Sue and Daphne. But they wouldn't take no for an answer.

"Alright. But I'm going straight home at midnight. OK?"

"OK, cried two voices in unison.

So off we went, two lively females and one moody individual who was determined not to enjoy herself.

I'd been seeing an American GI for a couple of months but he'd suddenly got a conscience about a girlfriend back home and decided it would be better if we didn't see each other. That could have been contributing to my melancholy mood, I guess. Rejection isn't easy to take in any circumstances. So I was fancy-free, but not likely to meet anyone that night I didn't already know. That was life in Rangoon. Same people, different location. How wrong could I have been?

As soon as we arrived at the party, I noticed a group of unfamiliar faces, all young men, an unusual occurrence in the small diplomatic community of Rangoon. My curiosity was aroused immediately, along with the rest of the females around me. Nothing much happened in Rangoon and when strangers appeared it was a big deal. But I still wasn't in the mood for socialising, so when one of them came over and asked me to dance, I politely rejected his offer and he moved on to the next young female who was happy to oblige.

However, this particular young man wasn't put off that easily, so when he asked me again, I accepted and quickly discovered that he and his friends were Merchant Navy officers from a ship called the *Barpeta*. They'd delivered an iced cone of flowers to the Australian Embassy for the Australia Day celebration on January 26.

The guy I was dancing with was the purser. His name was Clive.

"Why don't you join us?" he asked when the dance was over.

I still wasn't in the mood to make polite conversation, even if he was cute and handsome. I wanted to stay with my friends where I was comfortable. They didn't mind if I was a bit moody, we all got like that occasionally. However, Clive was very persistent and after two more dances, I agreed to join him at his table, probably because

I'd noticed that my 'ex' had arrived and was sitting there. Did I want to make him jealous? Of course, I did.

"Could I have the last dance?" Clive asked as the MC announced the last waltz. How could I refuse? I loved dancing and my mood had lifted. I was ready to bring in the New Year.

"This has been a great night so far. What now?" he asked as we took to the floor to the strains of *Could I Have This Dance for the Rest of my Life*. The universe was beginning to work its magic.

Back at the table, we were joined by Jacqui, from the Australian Embassy, and after the midnight celebrations, we decided to go back to her house and drink in New Year all over the world. So it was, that at 5.30 am on 1 January 1968, there were Merchant Navy officers crashed out all over Jacqui's house and the rest of us were saying – or was it shouting – Happy New Year to the UK. Some of the sailors were supposed to be on duty in a few hours. We couldn't wake all of them, but Clive and I managed to get a couple into my car and I drove them all back to the ship. No breathalysers in Rangoon. Thank goodness.

New Year's Day, 1968

I picked Clive up from the wharf the next evening and took him to an Italian Night at the British Club. There is no ladylike way to eat spaghetti, and it's especially embarrassing in front of a guy you've just met, but I was hungry and apparently he wasn't. He just watched me, enjoying my efforts to eat spaghetti gracefully. We were so comfortable together, I was beginning to feel a bit sad that he wasn't going to be around much longer. There was only one day left before he set sail again for India.

Next day, an invitation was delivered to the British and Australian Embassy staff to attend a party on board the *Barpeta*. I'd never been on board a ship before and we had a great time, dancing to Engelbert Humperdink's *Ten Guitars* and *There Goes My Only Possession* which would become our theme song for the next twelve months, along with *Honey I Miss You*. We met the captain and the rest of the officers, including those who'd spent the early hours of New Year's Day on Jacqui's floor, though I doubt any of them remembered us.

Their visit had certainly lifted my spirits and I was disappointed they were sailing the next day. They'd been in Rangoon for ten days and I hadn't noticed them until New Year's Eve – my own fault for being so miserable over the festive season. Apparently, I'd seen Clive at a Christmas Eve party, dancing with one of the American girls, but we were both unaware of each other. It was even more disappointing when he told me he was leaving the ship in Calcutta to go on leave, so wouldn't be with the *Barpeta* on its next trip to Burma in April.

Maybe it was the fact we were not likely to meet again that allowed us to talk freely to each other about our dreams for the future and our expectations of marriage and children. But, it was too late and too soon. Too late to see him again and it was too soon in a relationship to fall in love. Besides which, his fellow officers must have had good reason to call him 'Mrs Gandhi's Playboy'.

The following evening, as I was a having a lonely dinner, John answered the door and returned with a dozen red roses. I didn't know if it was Clive's writing, but it was his name on the card. I'd had a big enough problem myself trying to find someone to deliver flowers, and I lived there. I knew there certainly weren't any florist shops in Rangoon. So how did he manage that? Before he sailed that morning, Clive had somehow arranged to buy them, write a card and have them delivered to my address. How romantic! But I wouldn't be seeing him again, so I would just have to put him out of my mind. It wasn't easy. I couldn't help wondering where he was and what he was doing.

I didn't have to wait long.

★★★

A few weeks later a letter arrived. Sixteen pages, more like an essay than a letter, describing in detail the places he'd been and what he'd been doing. And the most important news of all, British India could find no one to replace him so he was on another trip and would be back in Rangoon in April. Excellent news. My heart was definitely singing.

I spent the two weeks prior to the arrival of the *Barpeta*, checking the shipping pages in the Rangoon Gazette. This was the most exciting time of my day and I would rush into the Chancery shouting "It's arriving at 1.30 pm on Tuesday." Or 3.30 pm and so on. When it finally did arrive, I had to wait for him to contact me. Would he? He would, wouldn't he? Had he forgotten? Would he really want to see me? I was a nervous wreck.

Then it happened. I walked out of the Embassy one afternoon after work and there he was, as handsome as ever in his white summer uniform. I hadn't seen him in uniform and he looked gorgeous. Crisp white shirt, with epaulettes, open at the neck with dark chest hair peeping through. And shorts.

We would have ten whole days together. Together maybe, but not alone. I soon found out that Clive was the organiser. He had somewhere to go but his shipmates seemed to depend on him for their entertainment as well. When I picked him up after work, I also collected four more officers and off we went to the Belfield Club for a meal and a drink, then back to my place for a nightcap. Or early morning cap.

We had an evening at the Club swimming pool where they all got drunk and proceeded to push each other into the pool. Wonderful! We were not used to such behaviour in our small community and the senior Embassy personnel at the pool were not impressed. Clive, not wanting his fellow officers to embarrass me, tried to intervene and got thrown in himself, fully clothed. That was the end of the party for us. I took him back to my place and left the others to find their own way home.

Pat and I had been hassling the Ambassador for invitations to the Queen's Birthday Party for all the officers on the ship. Their behaviour at the pool didn't help our cause. There was opposition from those who had witnessed their unruly conduct, and they made it quite clear that they did not wish to be embarrassed by a group of drunken louts in front of the rest of the Diplomatic community, at a serious British Embassy event. But His Excellency eventually agreed. It was a British ship after all and they were British officers. Their gentlemanly conduct would be assured by the presence of their Captain.

The evening was a success for everyone. A group of Merchant Navy officers in their dress uniforms was hard to resist and they were in demand all night for photo calls, especially from the ladies. And yes, they were well-behaved. I think they still had sore heads from the night at the pool.

The night before he left, Clive came over for dinner. Our first night completely on our own and I had it all planned, the meal, the wine, the music. I waited excitedly for his arrival, but, as he got out of the taxi, I could see that there was someone with him, a man and a woman. What now?

"Hi, doll. This is Oscar and his wife, Anne. They're on their honeymoon and have hardly been off the ship since we arrived, so thought it would be a good idea to bring them over to meet you. You don't mind, do you?"

Of course, I minded. But I tried to disguise my irritation, not something I'm particularly good at. John managed to stretch the meal to feed four of us but conversation was a bit strained, and not made any better by Clive starting to sing *There's a Kind of Hush*.... At least it broke the ice a little and we had a laugh about the situation.

"We seem to have interrupted your romantic evening," said Oscar.

What could I say? It was rather obvious that I'd planned the evening for two.

"Well, we haven't been alone much since the Barpeta arrived," I explained.

They both admonished Clive for his lack of sensitivity and, thankfully, the evening ended on a brighter note.

But, all good things must come to an end, and on the day of departure Pat and I asked His Excellency if we could go and see the ship off as it left at 10.00 am.

He smiled.

"Yes, please go and push it."

Although said in jest, he'd obviously had enough of our late nights and the tired young women who had been running his office for the last ten days.

So it was that we were standing on the quay, waving goodbye as the *Barpeta* moved slowly down the Rangoon River, carrying away the person I wanted to spend the rest of my life with, the words of Engelbert's current hit *There Goes My Only Possession* playing in my head.

But I'd be seeing him again soon. This time I was sure about that.

12

Is It Love?

**Rangoon-Calcutta-Bombay-Stanley-Bombay-Rangoon
May 1968**

Stay for another six months, go home, then another posting. To where? Or take six weeks leave and come back to Rangoon for another year. Any sensible person would have done the rest of the time, rather than spend an extra six months living with the restrictions imposed by Burma's military regime. But not me, not at that time. I was in love. There was no contest. I needed to see my handsome sailor again as soon as I could. Now I was lovesick as well as homesick.

So, I began to organise my UK leave. First stop? Calcutta. Where else? This was where Clive would be in May. This was where we would have time together – alone I hoped.

Suddenly, I was the most popular person in the Embassy. I was going back to the UK on leave and it seemed everyone wanted me to get something or take something. The Ambassador gave me a box of cigars to take to the US Ambassador at the American Embassy in London, the wife of a senior Attaché wanted me to buy her some material, some put in orders for records or other things they couldn't get in Burma, which amounted to just about everything. I was overwhelmed and didn't know what to do. I couldn't please everyone and I was terrified at being asked to choose material for a senior Embassy wife. So, I took the advice of a seasoned staff member and said no to everyone, except the Ambassador, of course, otherwise I would be spending all my leave shopping, with no room in my suitcases for my own wants and needs.

I left Burma on 12 May 1968 *en route* from Rangoon to Calcutta. I was a bit scared. It was only my second time on a plane and this was not Heathrow. Nobody looked at my boarding pass as I got on the plane and I sat waiting for take-off, hoping I was on the right flight and wondering if I should ask, or would I sound stupid? It's not like a bus, is it? They know where I'm going, don't they? I can hardly say, 'Excuse me, is this plane going to Calcutta?' or 'Can you put me off at the next stop please?' They'll think I'm crazy. All these thoughts were running through my head and I'd just decided to ask the name of the airport in Calcutta, a devious way of finding out if that's where we were headed, when I heard the word Calcutta over the loudspeaker. Hooray! I was on the right track or, to use the correct term, flight path.

"Please fasten your seat belts we are beginning our descent and will shortly be arriving at Dum Dum airport, Calcutta. The temperature is …"

I wasn't interested in the temperature. I couldn't wait to see him. Would he be there? Of course, he would. Then, those negative thoughts returned. There I was, in Calcutta where I knew no one except Clive, and I didn't really know him, did I? Why was I there? How did I get there? Questions I would be asking myself many times in the years ahead.

More thoughts kept crowding my head as I joined the other passengers walking across the tarmac to the airport building.

If he's not here what will I do? Plan B, I'll get a taxi to my hotel. Do they speak English here? The guys at customs don't seem to know much. Cigarettes? Yes, they're cigarettes. How many am I allowed? Too many? OK take them. No? OK, I'll keep them, just hurry up. Thank you.

Then he was there, giving me a hug, grabbing my suitcase, taking my hand and hailing a taxi. It was only a few weeks since we'd seen each other but it had seemed like a few years.

"Come on, get in, we're going to my uncle's place."

"Can we go to the hotel first so I can change?"

"Oh, no you're staying with me at my uncle's house. We'll cancel the hotel."

That was fine with me. I was happy to let him take control. I felt safe and I wanted to spend as much time as possible with him during my stay. But, not sure about the uncle.

I needn't have worried about that. His uncle wasn't around, but I met his cousin, Alan, and his girlfriend Ida. We had a wonderful first evening together at the Calcutta Yacht Club and next day we visited his father's grave. Clive was on leave in 1964 when his Dad collapsed in his arms and died soon after. It was a very sad story and I was touched that he'd taken me to the gravesite.

Next day we visited some of his friends, who all loved Jim Reeves and adored Clive. We had afternoon tea at Trinca's, a cafe with a quaint, old-fashioned atmosphere, where you could buy the most delicious and vast array of cakes and pastries. There was a dance floor and a band playing in the middle of the afternoon. Shades of the British Raj I think, except for the music, Cliff Richard, Jim Reeves, and Engelbert Humperdink being the most popular artists in India at that time.

Clive wanted my stay to be memorable, especially as he hadn't been able to take me on a proper date in Rangoon. But I had to spoil it all. I woke up one morning with a raging sore throat. Another bout of tonsillitis, the third since I'd left home. The American doctor in Rangoon had advised me to see a specialist when I was in London, to decide whether I needed to have my tonsils taken out before I returned to Burma. Not a nice way to spend my leave, and definitely not on my itinerary. Now, 50 years later, I still have my tonsils.

Clive took me to a doctor's surgery close to where we were

staying. I was given a penicillin injection and a prescription for antibiotics, but eating was not enjoyable. Every time I tried to swallow, it was so painful I kept squeezing Clive's arm. Not a good way to spend a romantic few days, but a great way to get to know each other better. He was very supportive and again I felt safe and protected with him. A good start.

So going out to dinner was not an option, but tonsillitis didn't stop me from hitting the shops, and getting there was an experience in itself. In the taxi on the way to the markets, we were stopped at traffic lights when, suddenly a hand appeared through the open, or more likely broken, window. I stifled a scream as I stared at a man's arm.

"Poor man. His arm looks like a lump of meat," I whispered.

"It probably is," said Clive, as he waved the man away with some choice words in Hindi. As I said, I felt safe and cared for, and the incident didn't affect my enthusiasm for a little retail therapy. I hadn't been able to buy anything but food and some Burmese craft pieces since I left England, so I had a great time wandering from shop to shop.

"Oh, look! They sell hot water bottles. Oh, they sell make-up and hair dryers."

You'd think I'd been locked away for years. Well, it had certainly seemed like it.

We were so relaxed and happy together and were able to learn more about each other's background. We talked about our childhood, education, school friends. There was so much we wanted to know and so little time.

Clive was born in Bangalore in the Southeast of the South Indian State of Karnataka in the heart of the Mysore Plateau. His family tree was much more interesting than mine. His paternal grandfather, along with thousands of his countrymen, had left Ireland for Liverpool during the potato famine and enlisted in the South Lancashire Fusiliers. After surviving the horrors of the First World

War he'd travelled to India to work on the railways, where he met and married the Portuguese woman who was to become Clive's grandmother.

His mother's parentage was also Portuguese and French, not unusual in India, which was colonised by Portugal and France in the 17th century, to increase their power in the spice trade. It's hard to believe that spices were once valued as highly as gold and silver, and people were willing to risk their lives by sailing to the ends of the earth in search of them. But good for me that they did.

The McCabe family spent the Second World War in Calcutta, eventually settling in Kanpur, the industrial capital of Uttar Pradesh, in 1947.

Even though we'd grown up in different countries and with a different cultural background, we discovered that we had so many things in common. There was never any money to spare in our families while we were growing up, so we discovered shared experiences of family hardship, and a strong emphasis on being the best we could be.

Our education was also similar. Clive was educated at La Martiniere College in Lucknow, an institute founded posthumously by Major-General Claude Martin, an officer in the French and later, British East India Company. In his Will, he stated that he wanted the building to be used 'for learning young men the English language and Christian religion, if they found themselves inclined'. It was an English education with exams equivalent to those I took at Bishop Auckland Girls' Grammar School, where I'd managed to attain three GCE 'O' levels, nowhere near the impressive eight 'O's and four 'A's Clive had achieved in his Senior Cambridge exams.

Strange, how fate plays such a big part in our lives. How did we end up together in Burma, and now Calcutta? After college, Clive had applied to the Central Board of Customs and Excise and was offered a position as a Customs Officer. However, a chance meeting with a friend of the family pointed him in another direction. Had he ever thought of a career in the Merchant Navy? British India Steam Navigation Company was recruiting. That sounded good too. So he gave it a try. Out of 1,500 applicants, only four were successful. Clive was one of them. My journey to this place, to our being together in Calcutta, was rather ordinary by comparison. A family move away from the town of my birth to a Golf Club in an unfamiliar part of the north-east, and a break up with a boyfriend of two years started a yearning to see more of the world. So here we were. Two people who had somehow managed to travel across the world to be in the right place at the right time.

We were so comfortable talking about ourselves, reliving our past through each other, but at the back of my mind, and his, was the question: how and when would we see each other again?

It had to end sometime, and I finally left Calcutta on 14th May. Next stop Bombay to see my friends from Rangoon, Bill and Liz Dixon. When they were on leave in England, they'd taken the time to visit Mam and Dad to give them some news of their daughter's adventures in Burma. I was looking forward to seeing them again and, as substitute parents, they were very anxious to hear more about this Indian fellow I'd been staying with in Calcutta.

I was beginning to feel quite a seasoned traveller as I boarded another plane. I'd stopped in Bombay on my way to Rangoon just over a year ago but only for an hour, alone in a rather unexciting airport. This time I hoped I would see a little bit of the city, and I had friends to meet me.

It was a joyful reunion with lots of catching up to do, especially as they hadn't met Clive and were looking forward to hearing more about him. Bill and Liz must have known then that I was totally hooked, as I monopolised every conversation with references to his sense of humour, or the way he winked or his organisational abilities. But they didn't know him, only what I'd told them and I could tell they were a little bit apprehensive about the situation.

I was only staying for two days but, as I'd expected, Bill and Liz wanted to show me around Bombay, so the day before I left, we took a short drive from their apartment in Prabhu Kutir, to admire the lush lawns and vibrant colours of the Hanging Gardens, so-called because of their position on the slopes of Malabar Hill. And Bill insisted that I couldn't leave Bombay without being subjected to the shocking and sometimes frightening experience of a car drive around a city where drivers and pedestrians each made their own road rules. Much the same as Calcutta really.

After such a stressful experience, we needed peace and quiet, and where better to enjoy a bit of that than in one of the tranquil restaurants of the magnificent Taj Mahal Hotel, where red-turbaned waiters hovered to cater to our every need. Over a hundred years old, the hotel was Bombay's first harbour entrance landmark, twenty-one years before the Gateway of India was constructed.

As the plane took off from Bombay on 19th May, for the final leg of my journey home, I had time to think about all that had transpired since I'd left. I'd been away for fourteen months and so much had happened to me. I felt I was living in a movie and couldn't wait to tell everyone about what I'd been doing during my time in Burma. We stopped at Zurich on the way to London and to my surprise, as I was wandering around the airport waiting for the boarding call, I heard my name over the loudspeaker.

"Will Valerie Dowson, come to the information desk, please. Valerie Dowson to the information desk."

What on earth was the matter? My insides were quivering with anxiety as I approached the counter and gave my name. A young woman handed me an envelope. As I opened it, I realised it was a card with the inscription, 'Wishing you a safe journey'. It was from Clive and he'd written 'If patience is the mother of virtue, I'm the father. Miss you.' How romantic could you get? And how had he managed to do that? I still don't know and now, as I write 50 years later, my dear husband can't remember. I was on Cloud Nine for the rest of the journey, my thoughts with the man I'd left behind and not the family I was about to be reunited with.

✯✯✯

I was met at the airport by Mam and Dad and Aunt and Uncle and we made our way to their home. But before I could go north I had a duty to check-in at the Foreign Office and talk to my boss and my friends in the Personnel Department. Of course they wanted to know how I was enjoying my posting in Rangoon. Then to the US Embassy to present the Ambassador with cigars from my Ambassador in Rangoon.

I arrived home on 20th May to a place I'd never seen before. The King's Head, Stanley had been home to Mam, Dad, and my sisters for about six months. It was strange for me, but it was still home. Home was where my family was and I was so happy to be there. And there were already two letters waiting for me from Clive. So I got to talk about him again, everything I knew and of course his background. Everyone wanted to know about his background.

Growing up in the North-east of England, I was educated in a Church of England environment, where the only information we thought we knew about Catholics was that they prayed to the Virgin Mary and pierced the ears of their baby girls. As teenagers, we knew we would never marry a Catholic and said it often. And it was very unusual to see foreigners in the north-east of England. Now, here I was, arriving home with pierced ears, done in Burma by the American doctor, and obviously besotted with a Catholic man from India.

I caught Mam looking at me with a not-quite-there smile.

"What's the matter, Mam?" I asked

"He's very special, this one, isn't he?" she said quietly. "I've never heard you talk about anyone else this way, even when you were engaged."

"Yes, Mam. He's very special," I replied.

I was engaged when I was 19 to a young man in the Royal Navy. I'm obviously attracted to sailors. A few months after our engagement, he was sent overseas and by the time he returned, we realised our relationship wasn't going to work.

Mam had been through my other love interests with me. She'd watched and cared for me in and out of all my relationships. She'd shared my joy when I was in love and hugged me when it fell apart. She knew me better than anyone else. So if she thought Clive was special, well, she was right.

28th May, 1968.

It was my birthday and I was twenty-four. It was great living in a pub, there was always a place to celebrate and I had a whole public house full of people to celebrate with. An enormous arrangement of flowers arrived during the day from ... guess who? I was definitely being wooed.

I managed to catch up with a couple of my friends. It had only been just over a year but I'd changed. Everyone around me at home was still the same and not really interested in Burma. I think it was too distant for most people to be able to relate to. Before I arrived there, I had no conception at all about the country so why would I expect my friends to? Having been away from TV all this time, I had nothing to add to conversations about local TV shows like Coronation Street and it didn't feel right to share my experiences, I was afraid of sounding a bit superior. I was out of touch and wouldn't be home long enough to catch up.

The 14th of June was Mam and Dad's 25th Wedding Anniversary. The world was still reeling from the shock of Bobby Kennedy's assassination in Los Angeles in the early hours of Thursday 6th June, and I could imagine the impact it would be having on my friends and colleagues in Rangoon. My sisters and I had been watching TV together when the news broke of John Kennedy's assassination barely five years before, and here we were again, and able to share our memories of that day. We were all in the same place at the same time, helping with the preparations for a family celebration. I didn't know it then, but it would be the last time I would see my extended family, my two grandmothers, uncles, aunts, and cousins, all together in one place.

In the midst of all the preparations and celebrations, Clive was always with me, in my head, and I couldn't wait to see him again. I'd received two more letters but I was a bit concerned about him. There had been a tragic train crash in India and I wasn't sure where he was. I knew he was going to Kanpur to help his family get ready for their move to Australia, but I couldn't remember on which days he was travelling, and not being able to contact him was frustrating and worrying.

Finally, a telegram arrived. He was OK. How thoughtful! He must have known I'd be worried. I didn't know when I would see him again, and in his last letter, he'd said he was still waiting for confirmation of his next ship. If we wanted to be together, how could we make that happen? He would be assigned to a ship going I didn't know where, and I was returning to Rangoon for another year. Then I could be posted to anywhere in the world. It was all too much to worry about. I had to leave it to fate. If it had to happen we'd find a way.

My leave was almost over and I prepared for departure with mixed feelings. I wanted to be at home, but I also wanted to be with Clive. I would have similar decisions to make in the future. But for now, the decision was made for me. I had to return to Burma for a year. But first, I would make another stop in Bombay and hope that Clive would be able to meet me there for a couple of days.

And so, on the 20th June, I arrived once more at Bombay airport, expecting to see Bill and Liz there to meet me. Surprise, surprise, there was Clive. *Unbelievable*! Fate had stepped in once more and made it clear that we were meant to be together.

In the taxi on the way to Bill and Liz's apartment I learned that he was in Bombay, waiting to pick up a ship in two weeks, sailing between Bombay and the Persian Gulf. And where was he staying? With Bill and Liz. He'd just rung the British High Commission, asked to speak to Bill, said who he was and could they meet. They did. He came, they saw, he conquered. He always managed to endear himself to people. Bill and Liz were obviously as smitten as I was, but perhaps not in the same way.

I was supposed to have six weeks leave and I'd already had five and a half. I'd only intended to stay in Bombay for a couple of days. But once again, fate was on our side. British Airways flight staff were on a 'go-slow' and some flights had been cancelled. There were problems getting onto flights to Burma. I could stay a little longer. But when Bill received a telegram from my boss, "Where's Twiggy?" I knew my time was up.

Bill finally managed to get me a seat on a flight to Rangoon on the last day of June, so I had two more days with Clive. He had lots of things to organise before he joined his ship, so the day before my flight, he went off on his own and promised to meet Liz and me at the Taj Mahal Hotel for lunch. We waited for an hour, wandering in and out of the shops within the hotel complex, but he didn't arrive. This is hard to understand in the current age of mobile phones when we're always in contact with each other. Then, we just had to be patient and wait for news, be it good or bad.

"I think someone's following us." I'd noticed the same man in or around all the shops we'd been into. We were two foreign women, alone in India.

"Let's get out of here," Liz decided, so we quickly hailed a taxi and went home.

We'd arranged to go out for dinner in the evening, our last time together for who knows how long. I just hoped he'd turn up and hadn't decided to desert me. He wouldn't do that, would he? I didn't think so, but doubts put into words by my friends back home came back to haunt me. You haven't known him long. You don't know anything about him. He could be a criminal. And they were right. What did I know about him? I knew enough to know that I wanted to spend more time with him, even the rest of my life.

I'd had a shower and had just finished putting rollers in my hair when there was a knock at the bedroom door.

"Come in."

The door slowly opened and a head appeared. Before I could say anything at all, he was down on one knee, with a ring box in his hand. He opened it up to display a three-sapphire engagement ring.

"Will you marry me?"

I still have that picture in my head of me seated at the dressing table, in a dressing gown and rollers in my hair. Not exactly my idea of how I would receive a proposal of marriage. Of course, my reply was a resounding "Yes!" He hadn't deserted me. But where had he been? Simple, he'd got held up with Indian government red tape. Paperwork!

We spent the rest of the evening contemplating our future. How would we do this? Would I be able to resign halfway through my posting? Would I have to refund any of the airfare that had been paid for me to return to Rangoon? When and where would we marry? There were a hundred things to be done but at that moment we were only thinking of us. We'd made the decision. We were getting married.

But we had to settle on a date and a place. It would be impossible to discuss this when I was in Rangoon and Clive was sailing up and down the Persian Gulf. So, next morning, with our heads a little clearer, we weighed the pros and cons of a wedding in the UK or in India. What was more important, getting married in the UK with all the expense that would entail for us and for my parents, or marrying in India where Clive had rupees he couldn't take out of the country? It was my choice to make. As Clive had already started the immigration process to Australia, it didn't make much sense for us both to travel to the UK to get married and then travel back to Australia. It was more sensible to save our money to help us settle in a new country.

Although I would have loved to return to the UK and show off my fiancé to my family and friends, I wasn't homesick at that moment. Home for me now was wherever Clive was. We wouldn't have to touch the money I'd saved as we could pay for the whole wedding in rupees. Bill and Liz had kindly offered to let us get married from their apartment and Bill would be proxy for my dad and give me away. Dad and Bill had met, so everything was working out well. We'd sail to Australia in January. At that stage in our lives nothing else mattered. It was settled. There would be a wedding in India on Wednesday, 18th December 1968. But first we had to return to work and let our employers know.

Another telegram arrived from Rangoon.

"Has Twiggy left Bombay yet?"

At this rate they'd send me back to the UK and all our plans would be ruined. It was painful leaving Clive at Bombay airport, but we would be together again in November. Four months. It seemed like a lifetime.

I arrived in Rangoon on 30th June with a ring on my finger, a smile on my face and my letter of resignation from HM Diplomatic Service. I was the second shorthand-typist in two years to resign for marriage reasons. They'd been correct when they'd told me in London that there was a high turnover of shorthand-typists in the Service.

But, as my status changed, so did my social standing in the diplomatic community.

13

I'm Backing Out

Rangoon, 1968

I have a new servant, a woman this time. My friends did the job I didn't want to do and replaced John with Orca. Although things had started out well with John, that was mainly because I didn't know what to expect from him. How could I? I'd never had a servant before. But friends had started commenting that he didn't stay around after a meal had been served. Apparently, he should have been there to pour drinks and clean up after everyone had gone. He always cleaned up in the morning, so this wasn't an issue for me. Until one morning, after a dinner party, I awoke to the mess from the night before and no breakfast. Where was John? There was no time to find out before work.

I arrived home at lunchtime to a clean house, but no lunch, just John holding up a bandaged index finger and a razor blade. He'd cut himself while cleaning my bathroom and was unable to work that day. Before I could decide what to do about this, Pat appeared. The other servants in the block had organised the cleaning of the flat and her servant, Maung Maung, had prepared lunch for both of us. This was teamwork before it became a corporate buzzword.

"John will have to go, Twiggy. He's not up to the job," my friends had told me before I went on leave.

I'd never had to hire or fire anyone before and I felt so sorry for him. He had a wife and I don't know how many children. Where would he go, I wondered, and how would he manage. The living quarters, such as they were, came with the job. Not my problem, I was told.

Having a woman in the flat made a big difference. Orca was so attentive, I realised what John hadn't been doing and I felt much more comfortable around her. Like many other servants, her story was one of hardship. She'd left her sick husband with her children in a small village, a few hours' walk from Rangoon. Once a month, she would spend her day off walking home to take them food and money and returning the next day the same way, on foot. So, although I was sad about John and his family, I was happy that I was supplying another family with the bare necessities of life. And Orca was always smiling. She had a job, and to her that was all she needed to be able to provide for her family.

After giving six months' notice of my intention to resign, I had to wait for approval from London. The Foreign Office could demand reimbursement of the fare they'd paid for me to return from the UK, but they couldn't keep me in Rangoon for the duration of my posting. And they didn't. In fact, the Ambassador had suggested that I be allowed to leave one month earlier to allow me time to organise the wedding. A wedding present from him, he said.

Inspired by the *I'm Backing Britain* campaign going on in the UK while I was there, I organised an *I'm Backing Out* party to announce my engagement and imminent departure from Rangoon. The British campaign was aimed at boosting the economy and was started by five secretaries who volunteered to work an extra half-hour each day without pay in order to increase productivity. I'd brought back some of their stickers and some London signs that I thought would be good for a theme party. I didn't know at the time that on my return to Rangoon I would be engaged to be married, so they came in very handy sooner than I'd expected. I was using them for a theme party, the theme being my engagement. Some of my friends who already knew about the engagement thought I was backing out of that, but no way. I was already counting the days to my departure. Four months seemed like four years.

Pat and I organised the invitations. The good thing about having parties in Burma was that we didn't have to do the hard work. We just purchased the necessities from the commissary and Orca and Maung Maung did the rest.

The party commenced at 3.00 pm and continued until the early hours. Looking at the photographs now, I wonder why I'm dressed in a white pleated tennis skirt and T-shirt – must have had a reason then. We're all looking hot and sweaty, a side effect of the monsoon season. It was wonderful to celebrate my engagement with all my friends, although a couple were very sceptical about the whole fairytale romance thing. Especially Dane, a marine who was so worried that I was going to get hurt that he called around every night for a week after the party trying to get his message across. The message, of course, was that I didn't know this person I was engaged to and fairy tale romances didn't last. But the underlying message was that I would be happier in America with him. Every day for a week after my return, a bouquet of roses arrived at the Embassy for me. The first was yellow. There was no note, but I knew they were from Dane.

"Thank you for the yellow roses," I said when I saw him that evening at the American Club.

"I didn't send you any yellow roses," he replied. "And I didn't send you any red ones either."

Sure enough, red roses arrived the next day and each day after. Seven days, seven bouquets of roses. It was flattering to know he cared enough to worry about me, but I had no qualms about my future with Clive. I'd already received three letters from him and I'd only been back for three weeks.

Yet things weren't all rosy in my life in Rangoon. After the party, I began to realise that I was not who I used to be anymore. I wasn't a single female, and I wasn't being invited to so many parties or dinners. I'd become invisible, socially anyway.

But, I was still very visible at work and our Ambassador asked if I would like to be married in Burma, he would be delighted and honoured to give me away. Now that would have been something to write home about. Definitely something for my parents to talk about at the Kings Head. But, sadly, I had to refuse his offer as we'd already decided that the wedding would be in Bombay with Bill and Liz, where we could use the money Clive wasn't allowed to take out of India.

Having been denied some input into my wedding plans, His Excellency (HE) decided that a contribution to my geographical knowledge of the country in which I had met my betrothed would have to suffice. I had to see more of Burma before I departed. The only place I'd visited outside of Rangoon was Sandoway, a small beach village about an hour's flight north, so he arranged for Pat and I to accompany him, and his wife, on a trip up country to Taunggyi, the capital of Shan State. My boss, who was the Counsellor and Chargé d'Affaires in the Ambassador's absence, came too. How would the Embassy survive without us for a week, I wondered. Well, HE said he wanted us to go, and he was in charge. So, including the driver, there were six of us in a four-wheel-drive bouncing along the roads to Taunggyi.

Did I enjoy this trip? Eventually, yes, it was great. But as we set off, I only wanted to be with Clive. Nothing looked particularly good or interesting without him. I should have been enjoying the journey and savouring all the wonderful features Burma had to offer, but I just kept wishing Clive was there. What a pain it must have been for Pat, having to put up with this unresponsive female beside her when she herself was so excited about her surroundings.

"Paddy fields and orchids. I don't ever want to see another paddy field in my whole life," I exclaimed to Pat as we opened the door of a small roadhouse where we'd stopped for the night.

"Have to agree with you there," Pat responded. "I'm first for the shower."

"Are you sure about that? Come and see this."

I was standing in the opening of a small alcove off the main room. There was no door, just a hose attached to a tap and a bucket. Maybe that was what constituted a double shower in Burma in those days. At least there was a toilet, but not a western one. It was one of those in the floor where you had to crouch down. I'd seen them before but never had to use one. What an experience!

Bedtime was an experience too, my first encounter with mosquito nets. We had to anchor the nets around our beds and then get in quickly and secure them. We did that very well, we thought and were just settling down when I heard that familiar buzz. Here I was, all tucked up in bed with a mosquito for company. I couldn't see it and didn't know where it was. With my history of adverse reactions to mosquito bites, there was no option but for both of us to get out of bed and start again. So, as I rearranged the net, Pat waved a sheet around my bed in the hope of blowing away any loiterers. At least we had a good laugh and we both survived the night without suffering any ill effects.

Arriving in Taunggyi, I was surprised when we stopped outside an English Tudor style cottage. We were on a plateau, with several similar cottages situated on the surrounding hillsides. Hearing our exclamations of surprise, His Excellency explained that these cottages were left over from the British occupation, when the administrative offices were moved from the shores of Inle Lake to the higher elevation, for health reasons. Taunggyi had also served as the chief garrison for military police and many of these old houses remained, some still occupied by their original residents. They looked so out of place but so picturesque and quaint in this small

Burmese town.

In spite of my melancholy disposition, I couldn't help but get excited about the markets in Taunggyi. It was impossible for me to understand how these poor people could produce such incredibly beautiful merchandise, especially the amazing fabrics in so many psychedelic colours and patterns. The vendors were almost as colourful as their goods and were definitely a great advertisement for their wares. I finally purchased enough exquisite emerald green silk with a going-away outfit in mind. I didn't know what I would find in India, but at least I now had one part of the wedding almost organised.

On another stall, I spied a long sword in a wooden scabbard. It was called a *dah* and there were two sizes, long and short. This one was a long *dah* and, with its red cord and orange-coloured wood, I couldn't resist it. I was sure Clive would love it. Was it bad luck to give someone a sword? We'd just have to wait and see.

On the way back to the car we came across a number of children in traditional dress, a picture of indescribable colours, sparkling and shimmering in the sunlight. We asked if we could take photographs and, to our amazement, they put their hands out for money "kyat" (chat), "kyat", they chanted in unison. So, we offered up the fee and posed them in groups for a photoshoot. Unfortunately, most of my film was water-damaged on the way back to Rangoon and to my great disappointment these photographs were lost forever.

The Ambassador took us to see his old friend who had stayed behind when the British left in 1948. He lived in one of the Tudor cottages on the side of a hill, and entering his house was like stepping back in time. There were photographs everywhere. All black and white and sepia, in large frames on the walls and in numerous small frames around the house, depicting people ranging from babies to older men and women, some posed in the customary style of that time, one sitting and one standing. Many of the men were in the full dress uniform of the British Army.

An elderly Burmese man, in the traditional dress of longyi and white shirt, so bent, his head was almost touching the teapot, brought us tea and fruit cake. I wanted to get up and take the tray from him in case he fell over and dropped it. But, he managed fine and backed out with a big smile, hands together in the old traditional way, not seen much amongst the younger Burmese people, many of whom had adopted the more western style of polite social behaviour.

Just as we were becoming used to the novelty of being able to wander around this town with its beautiful gardens and colourful markets, it was time to leave. Time to return to Rangoon with its restricted shopping and walking areas, where it was considered unsafe for us to walk anywhere alone.

The return trip to Rangoon was uneventful and Pat and I were not looking forward to getting back to reality. I'd enjoyed the break more than I'd imagined I would and I had a lot to write to Clive about. I was really glad I'd seen a bit more of Burma.

My Boss was leaving Rangoon too, and his replacement, Peter, was also adamant that I must see more of Burma, so, we took a trip across the Rangoon River to Syriam, now known as Thanlyin. The main point of interest there for Peter was the power plant, but for Pat and I, the candle and glass factories were much more appealing.

There were so many small temples in Syriam, with amazing statues of Buddha, chinthas, the guardian lions of the temples, and snakes. But the most incredible sight of our trip was the view from a temple over the river, where hundreds of catfish fought each other for the food offerings being thrown into the water by the locals. These fish are apparently sacred so people go there every day to feed them. How come I'd been in Rangoon for eighteen months and had never been to this place?

I was in good spirits as we boarded the ferry for the return trip and so grateful to HE for being thoughtful enough to take me to Taunggyi, and to my new boss for caring enough to bring me here. I was someone they hardly knew and would probably never see again after I left.

In October, my stay in Rangoon was almost over and I was suffering from mixed emotions. I was leaving people I'd worked with, cried with and had a lot of fun with. As well as my colleagues in the British Embassy, I had many happy memories of times spent with staff from the US and Australian Embassies. I knew I would miss them all. It was like leaving home all over again. But they too would be gone soon, back to their own countries and the friends and families they'd left behind. Or, unfortunately for some, back to Vietnam, to the fighting and the dying, to the horrors of a sad and useless war. It would be another seven years before Saigon finally fell to the North Vietnamese, and the troops would arrive home.

The last few weeks were spent packing up and shipping all my worldly goods to Australia. They would stay at a warehouse at the docks until we retrieved them. Now I was leaving, it didn't seem so long ago since I'd arrived and now I was doing everything in reverse. I would soon be in limbo again. I wouldn't see any of my effects until January when we arrived in Melbourne. It was all so emotionally exhausting and there wasn't really anyone I could talk to except Pat, and she'd been the recipient of all my emotional ramblings since she'd arrived. So I was alone most evenings. And what was there to be sad about anyway? I'd been wanting to leave ever since I got here. I had to learn to change my focus, especially as I had my wonderful man missing me as much as I was missing him.

My replacement arrived from the UK. An attractive mini-skirted young lady, much more confident than I'd been on my arrival. She would not only replace me in my job, she would also live in my flat, my home for almost two years. If I'd been feeling left out of things before, now I was definitely the invisible woman. This had to be one of the worst experiences of my life up until then. From being part of the 'in' crowd of the American, Australian and British Embassies, I was now sitting alone in my flat while everyone else was out somewhere enjoying themselves. The only people who seemed to remember I was still there were the wives of the Embassy UK-based staff. I was now one of them and no longer a threat.

But things got a little better when the farewell parties started and it was great to be able to say goodbye to everyone and receive their good wishes. The Ambassador gave me a send-off from his office where all the staff congregated to say goodbye and presented me with a beautiful beaten silver rose bowl. Even the owner of the small jewellery shop where I'd bought cufflinks for Clive's wedding present and had earrings made from some pieces of jade bought in the local markets, had given me some silver napkin rings. These gifts, along with a small box of silver teaspoons with chinthas on the handles, from one of my American friends, Dave, helped to ease the ache in my heart on leaving this place that I'd been trying to get away from for so long. Now I realised that it was the people I was going to miss, not the place. The people who had watched me mature from a naive young girl who didn't know which cutlery to use, into an independent woman about to be married.

Not surprisingly, leaving Orca was the most difficult. She'd been with me for such a short time but had become a friend and she cared for me like a mother. On the morning of 11th November 1968, neither of us could hold back the tears as we hugged each other goodbye.

"You be happy with your man. I be OK," she sobbed.

"You be happy too. I'll miss you," I whispered as I emptied my purse of Burmese currency and pushed it into her hand. I wouldn't be needing it again, and 70 kyat, more than three months' wages, would seem like a fortune to her.

At eight o'clock I arrived at the airport with Pat and was disappointed, but not surprised, that no one else had come to see me off. The night before had been the annual Marine Ball so most of the Americans would still be asleep. This time last year, I had an escort, a corsage and was driven to the event in a black limousine. But this time last year I hadn't met Clive.

On the plane I broke down, I couldn't stop the tears and the poor hostess didn't know what to do with me. It seemed like I'd been crying for a week. Again I was leaving a place that had been home to me for almost two years and it was hard to just say goodbye without reflecting on the good times.

14

A Wedding in India

November-December, 1968

A familiar, damp smell of humidity, disinfectant, and incense, unique to Bombay airport, assailed me as I entered the building, smiling at the thought that when I left Bombay I'd be Mrs Clive McCabe. I could feel the excitement beginning to stir in me. But that was six weeks ahead and there was a lot to do before then. It was all a bit daunting. Invitations, reception, wedding dress, cake and all to be organised by me in an unfamiliar country and an even less familiar language.

This time there was no Clive to meet me, he was on another ship, the *Sirdhana*, sailing between Bombay and the Persian Gulf, a three-week turnaround. He was due back in Bombay in three days and then would do one last trip before returning to Bombay on 12th December, six days before our wedding on the eighteenth.

The last time I was here, I didn't have time to take in the whole atmosphere of the country, I was more interested in where Clive was, rather than where I was. Now, without that distraction, I decided to find out more about the country where my future husband was born and especially the city where I was soon to be married.

Bombay, now known as Mumbai, lies on the west coast of India and is the capital of the state of Maharashtra. Millions of people live or merely exist here, in dwellings ranging from modern apartment buildings to sprawling slums on the city outskirts. In 1968 there was a caste system operating which was much more obvious than anything I'd seen in Burma. Although Bill and Liz had servants, these people didn't touch the toilets. A woman came in just to clean them. And even the servants in the house were part of a hierarchy from the chief bearer and cook down to the young woman who swept the floor and did the washing.

As in Burma, there was a club for foreigners in Bombay called Breach Candy, where membership was not restricted to the Diplomatic Community. But to my surprise, it was restricted to white people only. I found that very hard to understand, that the people who lived there, the Indian people themselves, were not allowed into this establishment. I believe this has now changed, but in 1968 it was still the case.

✯✯✯

Sitting on the balcony of Bill and Liz's third-floor apartment at Prabhu Kutir, I waited for a taxi bringing my sailor back to me. I'd rung P & O three times and they kept saying yes, the ship would arrive today. Every day I got the same answer. It was a bit like talking to some of the airport staff in Burma, who would read religiously from the flight timetable, even though the plane was six hours overdue. Anyway, Clive finally called and was definitely on his way.

"He's here, he's here," I shouted, only to realise that the arm hanging out of the taxi window didn't belong to Clive. This happened a few more times, and of course, I had to be right eventually.

The next three days were so hectic. We had to make a start on the wedding arrangements, but the most important decision to be made was where the ceremony would take place. Clive was a Catholic and I was a Protestant and we both definitely wanted to get married in a church. However, although Clive was not what they call a 'practising Catholic', he still wanted any children we might have to be brought up in the Catholic faith.

Well, I didn't know much about the Catholic faith and, as I was getting married far from home with no relatives attending, we decided that we should marry in a Church of England church and think about the children if and when they happened. So we went together to All Saints Church on Malabar Hill in Bombay and arranged to have the banns read for the next three weeks. Our Minister, Alwyn Jones, was Welsh. With a smile on his face, he told us he had held funeral services recently but it was a long time since he had been in charge of a wedding.

"There's a marvellous organist," he said. "It's Mendelssohn when you arrive and 'Here Comes the Bride' when you leave, isn't it?" We made sure that he had the correct order and arranged for the banns to be read at the church for the next three weeks. The purpose of calling the banns is to inform the community of an intended marriage, in order to prevent the unlawful union of two people. I doubt there would have been anyone in Bombay, apart from those in the High Commission, who even knew us, let alone have been able to cite any impediment to our lawful union.

We didn't expect to have many guests, most would be from the British High Commission and Clive's fellow officers from the ship, so the reception was easy enough to organise. We'd dined at The Ambassador Hotel in Bombay a few times and they were delighted to cater for us at the home of good friends Bill and Dorothy Horton, colleagues of Bill and Liz.

I had a list of his relatives and friends so, when Clive left for his last trip as a Merchant Navy Officer, I only had to find someone to make a wedding dress, a going-away outfit, a wedding cake and have invitations printed and despatched. Easy. Wedding cake, no problems. I found a bakery, looked at a few photographs, removed some of the flowery bits and done. It would be ready to pick up in two weeks.

Then, the wedding dress. Liz had a Simplicity pattern book, always a must for Diplomatic females living in Asian countries, as suitable off-the-rack clothes were not as easy to find there as in the UK. But there were always talented dressmakers to be found.

I decided on a straight, floor-length dress with long sleeves, very intricate embroidery around the neckline and a detachable train, and Liz took me to her dressmaker where I chose a white, Thai silk fabric. When I went back for a fitting I was a bit disappointed that it looked more off-white than pure white, but it was still beautiful. Although white veils were not traditional in India, my dressmaker managed to find some white net to which she attached a tiara of white silk flowers and pearls. I was impressed and thankful that was another part of the process finished. Nine-year-old Susan, Bill and Liz's daughter, was my bridesmaid so we needed a dress for her too. Then there was only the going-away outfit to organise and my emerald green Thai silk, bought in Taunggyi soon became a beautiful straight mini shift dress.

Finally, invitations were sent off to our relatives and friends in India, Burma, Australia, and the UK and soon it was 11th December and I was getting worried.

I'd called P & O twice and they kept giving me a different day. The *Sirdhana* was definitely not going to be here on the twelfth. And we had a major problem. I'd just been told that the banns had been called only once. We'd gone together to the first calling but since Clive had sailed, and with all the preparations, I had forgotten completely.

Because the banns hadn't been called, Clive needed to be here at least 48 hours before the wedding so that we could find a Canon who would give us permission to get married. We needed a special licence to marry.

Then another major catastrophe presented itself. There would be no spirits available for our wedding. The state of Maharashtra has a prohibition policy which restricts the sale and consumption of alcohol, but this doesn't apply to members of the diplomatic staff who are allowed to purchase alcohol duty-free. The Indian State and Excise Department had decided to prohibit the import of alcohol to members of diplomatic missions in Bombay for the month of December. For us, that meant no alcohol at our wedding. So much for Frank Sinatra's *Fly Me to the Moon*. There were definitely no bars in old Bombay, not unless you were an alcoholic. What there were, were Permit Rooms, and to enter a permit room you had to have a permit. Members of the diplomatic community didn't need a permit, their passports were enough, but, as an Indian National, Clive had to get a medical certificate from his doctor to say he was an alcoholic. In the eyes of the Indian Government, I was marrying an alcoholic.

So, at this point, the banns hadn't been called, there was no alcohol for our wedding, Clive was somewhere on the high seas and I didn't even know if he'd be in Bombay in time for the wedding. What else could happen?

It's difficult to understand in this age of mobile phones and internet, that making a phone call between countries could sometimes take twenty-four hours to arrange and in Asia and the Middle East it was almost impossible. I knew if he could get a message to me he would. For the moment I just had to wait. And wait.

Another couple of days passed without news. It was now the 16th of December and I was getting really worried. I got a letter from my Aunt Agnes and Uncle George in England, my second family. Uncle George wrote that they'd love to come to the wedding, "but you can't depend on the buses these days." His sense of humour in the midst of my dilemma made me nostalgic for home. Why was I getting married miles away from all my loved ones? This wouldn't be happening if we'd decided to go back to the UK to get married. I didn't want to cry because Bill and Liz were being so wonderful, and I didn't want to appear ungrateful. I hid myself in my bedroom and then, in the midst of my misery Liz shouted through the door.

"Twiggy, Clive'll be here in a couple of hours. Do you want to go down to the wharf to meet him?"

Did I? Of course I did! As the ship pulled slowly into the dock, there he was standing on the deck. And there we were, Bill and Liz and Susan and me, shouting:

"The banns haven't been called."

"We have to go find a Canon."

"We don't have any booze for the wedding."

He just laughed. He thought we were joking.

But, as soon as he understood what was going on, Clive took over with his usual no-nonsense approach. We set off immediately for the Seamen's Mission to ask who we could get to issue a marriage licence, then took a taxi straight away to the Canon's house and got the licence. Whew. No messing around. He'd only been ashore for two hours and we had already solved the most important problem.

Now for the alcohol. Next stop an Indian bottle shop. In this state of prohibition, you wouldn't expect to see a bottle shop, but of course, alcoholics have to buy their booze somewhere. Clive used his piece of paper to prove his status as an alcoholic and, together with my diplomatic passport, we managed to purchase Indian beer. Bill had saved some champagne from our engagement in July so we had at least enough for a couple of toasts, and their wonderful friends at the High Commission got together and promised to donate a bottle of spirits each. My hero was back and all was well with the world.

That same night, Clive hosted his bachelor night on the ship, but he wasn't sleeping on board. He'd decided to come back to Prabhu Kutir because he had now officially resigned from the Merchant Navy. Having seen a few bridegrooms looking very green and seedy at their weddings, I was a bit concerned, so spent most of the night waiting for his return. I needn't have worried. I was quite surprised when he appeared, looking as sober as when he had left.

"Well," he said. "I had to look after the bar. I'm the one who was paying for the booze."

Of course. How sensible.

✯✯✯

Wednesday 18 December 1968. My wedding day. I stood in front of the mirror in my bedroom, a young woman dressed in white, about to embark on a journey which would change her life forever. But the bride in the mirror looked sad, my thoughts turning to home and family. In an hour I would be married. In a foreign country. Not the wedding I'd dreamed about, with Dad at my side, tall and proud, my sisters as bridesmaids, just as we'd always dreamed they would be, and Mam in a new suit and a big hat. The suit would have been blue, pale blue. She always looked good in blue, with her blue eyes and fair hair. No, I'd be walking down the aisle with Bill, a good friend, but not Dad; Bill's wife Liz in a smart suit and a big hat, but not my Mum; their daughter, Susan, my bridesmaid, but not the two bridesmaids I had imagined, not my sisters, not Olwyn and Carol.

I was dragged out of my reverie into reality when Bill appeared in the mirror beside me, offering a handkerchief. I'd been staring into the mirror, into my imagination, looking back at my childhood and how I'd arrived at this place in my life, when I realised that even though I had Bill and Liz and the man I was about to marry, really, in my head, I was still alone. Without my family, there was no one to reminisce with, no one to tell funny and embarrassing stories about me. Even Clive didn't really know me, nor I him.

Lost in my thoughts, I'd been unaware of the tears streaming down my face.

"Well, doesn't everyone cry on their wedding day?" I murmured as I took the handkerchief from Bill

Liz and Susan had left for the church and Bill and I were alone.

He looked at me, all dressed up in my finery.

"Twiggy, your dad would be so proud of you. In his place, let me give you some advice. In every relationship, there'll be arguments and disagreements. If there are no disagreements, someone is lying or afraid. You are individuals and you have individual opinions. Never lie and never be afraid. Be yourself."

Of course, that released more tears. But there was no time for such self-indulgence, the car had arrived and it was time to go. Bill had organised the vehicles. I'd expected an ordinary sedan, no frills, so I was surprised when I reached the bottom of the stairs and saw the ribbons and streamers of fragrant jasmine flowers covering a black limousine, the only sign that this was a wedding in India. What a lovely gesture.

All Saints was a beautiful little church which could have been set somewhere in the English countryside. Perfect for an English bride. I walked down the aisle, looking straight ahead at Clive who had turned to watch me. As we said our vows, his voice boomed out so loudly I was sure the surrounding shopkeepers would have been able to participate in the service. As for me, I had no voice. I was so nervous, it was almost a whisper, and I was worried that I would start to giggle, which seemed to happen to me at the most serious and inappropriate times.

Apart from the vicar telling us to go and sit down, and then stand up again as he'd forgotten some of the service, everything went well, until he stepped on my train as he followed us down the aisle. Another moment in time not shared by my family. This should have been a special day for them too. But, again I had to tell myself that this was my choice. I walked out of the church into the Bombay sunshine, and as the photographer snapped a photo of me leaning over to kiss my husband, the smile on my face shouted to the world that I was the happiest girl on the planet.

At the reception, I hardly knew anyone. I'd never met any of Clive's fellow officers from the *Sirdhana*, nor his best man, but there were a few people from the British High Commission who looked familiar. The speeches were made and Bill did a wonderful job in the absence of my own Dad. After all he knew things about me that Dad didn't – the Diplomatic Community in Rangoon was very small. We danced the bridal waltz to the Hawaiian Wedding Song and then it was time to get changed and go off to our hotel, the *Sun'n'Sand*. The bride and groom didn't hang around very long in those days. The guests had just started dancing our favourite dance, The Slop and I remember thinking that we were missing out on the fun of our party. Nowadays, the happy couple stay until the end and are farewelled by a circle of guests. As a woman who loves to dance, in my opinion that's a much better way to conclude the wedding reception.

Unfortunately, the High Commission hadn't been able to organise my new passport in time and, arriving at the hotel, there was a bit of a problem. I was booked in as Mrs Clive McCabe and my passport stated that I was Miss Valerie Dowson. From the look on the faces of the hotel staff at reception, I was convinced they thought we were pretending to be married so that we could indulge in unsavoury practices in their hotel.

But after Clive produced our marriage certificate, they apologised profusely and we were escorted to our room. As we opened the door, the first thing we saw was a large notice on the dressing table saying that we had to leave the room at five in the morning as the pest control people were coming at half-past five to spray. *Ha Ha. Very funny.* So, we put the Do Not Disturb notice on the door and forgot about it.

Opening our suitcases, we found more evidence that our 'friends' had been at work – hundreds of tiny, paper circles from a hole-punch covered the contents. They couldn't buy confetti in India, so they'd filled our suitcases with something similar. And a magnum of champagne. There we were, in a hotel in the State of Maharashtra where you could only consume alcohol in a permit room, with a licence, and now we had a magnum of champagne to get rid of without getting caught. What could we do with it? I didn't fancy spending part of my honeymoon in an Indian police cell. So, in the absence of champagne glasses, we used tumblers from the bathroom and drank to each other until it was all gone. There was no way we'd be up at five-thirty after that.

Next morning, we were aroused from our alcohol-induced slumber by the hotel housekeeping staff. It was 10 o'clock. We dressed quickly and hurried off to find breakfast, leaving two startled maids to wonder how hundreds of tiny pieces of paper came to be scattered across the bedroom carpet. As we passed the reception desk, we were informed that the pest controllers had indeed tried to wake us, but to no avail.

The *Sun'n'Sand* was a popular hotel in Bombay, especially as a stopover for flight crews. Clive hated sunbathing. His constant cry was, "If this is your idea of fun, it's certainly not mine". So I acquainted him with one of Mam's favourite expressions – *savage amusement.*

But he didn't mind the view around the swimming pool, as British Airways' hostesses donned their bikinis to get a bit of sun before returning to an English December.

We managed to smuggle our empty champagne bottle out of the hotel a week later and soon we were in the midst of Christmas and New Year's Eve parties. Then, the ship to Australia.

15

Voyage to the Future

January-February 1969

Clive's shipping company very kindly allowed us to travel free to Australia on the cargo-passenger ship *Chandpara*. We paid victualling rates, meaning that we only had to pay for our meals. That was a great help as we didn't have to dip into our savings for airfares.

So, after a rather noisy, alcoholic party on board, we said farewell to our friends, hello to the other passengers and set sail from Bombay on 29th January 1969. We'd be calling at Cochin, a short trip down the coast from Bombay, Colombo, and Trincomalee in Ceylon, then full steam ahead to Australia, a four-week voyage to our future together.

Life onboard a cargo-passenger ship is very different from one catering for passengers only. A cargo-passenger ship has no extra amenities, no entertainment, no swimming pools. We had to amuse ourselves, so it was pretty important to be able to mix with the others on board. We all took our meals in the same dining room as the ship's officers and while at sea, we spent most of our time in the passenger lounge, playing cards, board games or Scrabble and drinking rusty nails – a cocktail of whiskey and Drambuie. Just a continuation of the pattern of my life in Rangoon and Bombay really. There was also a small library which for me, an avid reader, was a real blessing. I spent many an afternoon absorbed in the imaginary world of books while Clive was in the bar socialising with the other passengers, or with some of the ship's officers. Sandra and David Tickell were among the passengers on board and we spent much of our time with them and their five-year-old son, Quinton. They had travelled from England to India and were now on their way to New Zealand.

Cochin was our first stop, but we weren't allowed to disembark there and we only had time to buy a few trinkets from the young boys who circled the ship in their small boats. How they stayed afloat was a mystery to us all.

Ceylon, now known as Sri Lanka, was next and we dropped anchor away from the dock. This meant we had to make our way down a swaying rope ladder and step into a very unstable, rocking lifeboat. I was petrified. My stomach was doing somersaults as I gingerly took each step and then had to almost jump into the lifeboat where I fell into the waiting arms of one of the ship's officers.

Once ashore in Colombo, we headed for the shops and, after purchasing a few souvenirs, joined Sandra, David, and Quinton on a trip to Kandy. We'll never forget that ride. It was so bumpy, we were constantly moving in our seats for most of the hour it took us to get there. We had tea in the Queens Hotel, originally a Governor's mansion, and very reminiscent of the British Raj, with its old-fashioned ceiling fans slowly circulating, but providing little relief from the oppressive heat. Even the patrons of this establishment looked as if they'd just stepped out of the pages of a history book, women in their long dresses, carrying parasols and men in their fancy waistcoats. And this was real life, not a fancy dress party. Some of these diners had lived in Kandy since the end of World War II when the South East Asia Command of the allies was stationed there. Another sign of how special Asia had been to the British.

White-liveried waiters with gold turbans delivered three-tiered plates with tiny cakes, pots of tea, slices of lemon and jugs of hot water, reappearing at our sides the moment the last sip of lemon tea was taken. Definitely a taste of days gone by.

After tea, we visited The Temple of the Tooth, so-called because it houses the Relic of the Tooth of the Buddha, brought from India in 371 AD and is one of the holiest places of worship and pilgrimage for Buddhists around the world. We didn't actually see the tooth as the Temple was closed to visitors that day, but it was a fascinating end to a very interesting day out in Kandy.

We sailed around to Trincomalee, a place where Clive once got so sunburnt he stood in the shower and scrubbed his skin until it peeled. Ouch! So I took great care to stay in the shade. But some were not as sensible, and at dinner time we were three passengers short as the others writhed in agony on their bunks, looking like lobsters straight out of the pan.

From Trincomalee, the voyage got a bit rough in more ways than one. Although Clive and I had known each other for a year, we'd actually been in each other's company for only twenty-six days. We knew that many of our friends in Burma and India thought it wouldn't last. A couple living a carefree existence in Asia with servants to look after them had not lived in the real world together. How could such a marriage survive?

It was true, we knew very little about each other and so we were now on a huge learning curve, travelling together into the unknown. I had a new husband and I was off to a new country to meet new people. A bit scary really. But Clive was in the same situation – he also had a new partner, though at least he was familiar with Australia. He'd sailed around the Australian coast numerous times during his ten years as a Merchant Navy Officer and he had friends and family there.

We began to learn about each other very quickly. Our first argument was over my calling everybody 'love', just a North-country greeting or acknowledgment tag. However, to Clive it was totally wrong for me to be saying 'Thanks, love' to his friend, the purser. This was a difficult habit to break so I decided that the less I said the better. Then he thought I was sulking. Oh dear!

Another incident which caused a problem between us was the 'crossing of the line'. Anyone who hadn't crossed the equator had to go through a sort of initiation ceremony. I was the only passenger who hadn't done this and I was not about to get into a swimsuit and have wet fish slapped over me by a group of Merchant Navy officers. Clive was not impressed and felt, as the wife of a Merchant Navy officer, I'd embarrassed him.

However, the weather made sure that we couldn't be angry with each other for long. The boat was rocked quite violently every night, so we had to sleep very close together in one bunk with a pillow on the edge to stop us falling off. At least I wasn't seasick, an illness that seemed to afflict most of the passengers. We were often the only two passengers at the captain's table for dinner. Thank goodness, I thought, I've redeemed myself a little. I don't know how Clive would have coped with his wife being seasick as well as unsociable.

Just before we reached Fremantle, the officers held a party in their Mess. We both loved dancing and hadn't had much opportunity to dance together since the night we met, so we were looking forward to this event. Unfortunately, it didn't turn out quite as well as I'd expected.

During the evening while Clive was at the bar, I happily accepted an officer's invitation to dance. It didn't occur to me that Clive might be annoyed. But he was. I could see him looking at me across the room. I waved. He turned around and left. I waited a few minutes after the music finished and then made my way back to the cabin. He was there, waiting for me. He told me that I was married now and couldn't carry on as I did before. As a married woman, a man had to get my husband's permission to ask me to dance. What century were we living in? I had married a gentleman and he expected every other male to be one too.

His jealousy made me quite worried and nervous, especially when we were in mixed company. When I was sixteen, I had a boyfriend who was very possessive and jealous. I hadn't known Clive long enough to know his deeper personality. I knew he was well-liked by everyone who knew him but they didn't have to live with him. What had I got myself into? I wondered.

I needed to find a place to be alone and think about being a wife. What did Clive mean about not carrying on as I did before? I hadn't been aware that I was 'carrying on', which in my mind means flirting. Was I doing that in Burma? I think not. But in Clive's eyes maybe I was. You had to have lived in the Rangoon Diplomatic Community to understand the familiarity generated by the hours, days, months and years of working and socialising in close proximity.

The Vietnam War was a traumatic time for Americans everywhere and especially for the GIs and the Marines in Rangoon who had friends and colleagues still fighting there. Often, they just needed someone to talk to, but in the '60s very few people believed that a platonic relationship could exist between members of the opposite sex.

I started to understand how Clive had seen the bond I shared with some of the guys as flirting. It would take a while to show him I was not a flirt, just a compassionate young woman who had shared their pain. A hug and kiss on the cheek was a sisterly act on my part and certainly not flirtatious. Nor was it taken as such by the people who knew me, and I was well protected by these men. Their presence had made me feel safe and respected.

But those were unusual circumstances. This was the real world and it was time to step out of the fantasy and become real if we were to move on with the commitment we'd made to each other. We had a good basis for a successful marriage. We had the same values, we believed in the same things and, although we were raised in extremely different environments, our upbringing was very similar.

★★★

As we approached Fremantle in Western Australia, I began to get a bit nervous. I was about to meet Clive's family, his mother, sister, brother-in-law, and three children. Most new wives had time to get to know their future in-laws before the wedding, I didn't know what to expect. His family had migrated to Western Australia the previous May and as we were only in Fremantle for the day, they were going to meet us, take us to their house and then bring us back that evening.

However, when we disembarked there was no one waiting for us. The sister of one of the passengers offered to take us into Perth and we got a taxi from there. We arrived at a small bungalow in Mt Lawley and knocked on the door. There was no one home. Of course not, they would be waiting on the dock for us. I followed Clive to the back of the house where he was on his knees in front of the back door.

"What are you doing?"

"Got it." He held up a key, smiling as he opened the door. "Old habits."

Inside, I felt like an intruder, worried I might be caught trespassing.

"Do you want a sandwich?" he asked.

"No, thank you. We can't take food from your sister's fridge when she's not home."

"Of course we can."

A little later, we heard voices outside.

"Where's the key, hon?"

"Have you got the key, dearie?"

"Oh, the door's open. Is that you, Clive?"

So, when the family arrived home, there was I, munching on a cheese sandwich like I belonged there. Which I did, I suppose.

It was great to finally meet them, but it only made me more

homesick for my own family. I was here with his family but mine still hadn't met my new husband. During the past eight months, I'd been engaged, married, sailed halfway around the world with a man I hardly knew and my family hadn't even met him yet. I had to keep telling myself that this was my choice. Of course I was homesick. That was natural for someone so far away from home. I would soon be settled in a new home with my new husband. I'd be too busy to be homesick.

Back on the ship, we settled down for the week-long trip across the Great Australian Bight to Sydney. I was looking forward to our new life in Melbourne, totally unprepared for the emotional journey which lay ahead of me.

16

Love Hurts

Melbourne, 1969-1970

Standing on the deck as we approached Sydney Harbour, I joined in the exclamations of delight. This was a magical experience, the beginning of another adventure, a time of discovery in a different country, its nature, its environment, its climate, and its people.

It was early evening as we moved slowly towards The Heads and as the light faded, ahead of us appeared the famous Sydney Harbour Bridge and to the left, the as-yet-unfinished, magnificent Opera House.

"Look at the lights," someone shouted. Then everyone started oohing and aahing and shrieking with excitement.

"We have electricity in England as well," I murmured.

Now where did that come from?

I felt an arm around my shoulders. "You're missing home, aren't you, love?"

Fighting to hold back the tears, I turned to Sandra.

"Yes. A bit," I murmured.

And I was also a little disturbed that my mood could change so quickly; from excitement about the future to nostalgia about the past in the space of a few moments. My homesickness was already becoming a problem, but I didn't know that at the time. I thought it would soon pass, as it had in Burma. At least Sandra understood. She was on her way to New Zealand with her husband and son and was also a long way from her family and friends. I didn't want to spoil this experience for the others, so I tried very hard to suppress my feelings of isolation by putting a smile on my face and hearing Mam's advice in my head.

"Now, our Valerie, if you can't say anything nice, then don't say anything."

But how was I to know that this would not pass quickly? This was a symptom of something much deeper. Suppressing my feelings and my thoughts was already beginning to change my personality.

We were supposed to catch a train for the last leg of our journey but we 'd arrived in Australia during a period of growing industrial unrest. Hundreds of workers across the country were on strike, including Sydney train drivers. So, after an unscheduled night in a hotel, we managed to get on a coach to our final destination, Melbourne, the capital of Victoria. Ready or not, this was my new life.

After a couple of nights in a hotel, we moved into a furnished flat in South Yarra and I soon found work as secretary to the Insurance Manager of Trans Australia Airways, with an ulterior motive – cheap fares home. But there was a catch. I had to work there for at least a year and then I might have to give up my seat for a full fare-paying passenger, so I would always be on standby. But it was my first job and I was so excited to be working again. I was 'up, up and away with TAA'. That was the jingle for TAA's TV commercial in 1969.

This was where I encountered my first problem in Australia; taking dictation from my boss. As anyone who has used shorthand knows, the structure and placement of the outlines are based on pronunciation. We spoke the same language but in a different way. When he said 'main' I heard "mine", "claim" became "climb" and "mail" became "mile". Most words were obvious from the context of the document but I still seemed to be constantly in his office, reading out sentences or asking him to repeat a particular word. Fortunately for me, my boss had a great sense of humour and his accent, together with my limited knowledge of insurance vocabulary, made for an interesting and entertaining start to my secretarial career in Australia.

Overseas Containers Limited (OCL) was a fairly new company, formed early in 1969, and like British India Steamship Navigation Company, was part of the P & O group. With Clive's background in shipping, it made sense to try them first. It paid off, and he was soon employed as an import officer. The service was inaugurated on 6 March 1969 with a ship named *Encounter Bay* and we were fortunate enough to be invited on board the vessel in Melbourne, to celebrate its inaugural voyage from Australia.

Things were going well. We both had jobs, with decent wages. Well, Clive's was a decent wage because he was a man. I was earning about $40 per week as a secretary compared to his $75 as an import clerk. To me, the duties were quite similar, and I thought that my shorthand, typewriting, and secretarial diploma would count for something more. But this was 1969, and I was a woman.

We were paid in cash which came in small brown envelopes, personally delivered to us at our desks – real money which we could spend immediately. This was before credit cards, EFTPOS and the hole in the wall bank. The only reason we entered a bank was to deposit money. We had a small bank book where all deposits and withdrawals were handwritten, but we rarely needed to withdraw money. No passwords to remember and no waiting for cheques to clear. The simple life.

I enjoyed working at TAA but the pay was lower than some of the other jobs around. I'd given up the idea of cheap fares home as I didn't fancy travelling to the UK with a chance of being stranded in Singapore, so I started looking for another place to work. This time I used an employment agency, Drake Personnel, a new concept for me. My previous jobs had always required a letter of application, followed by an interview and a letter of offer which could take up to a month. At Drake, I just had to show up, have a chat and attend an interview the same day. As the job was in the accounts department there would be a lot of figure typing, so I was asked to type a table of numbers with four carbon copies, a mammoth task in those days of manual typewriters. It involved arithmetic; adding the number of characters in each column, taking them away from the number of characters which could fit on the page and dividing the remainder by the number of spaces between the columns, then setting the margins. And that was the easy part. There was also the typing of the table lines and the procedure for erasing errors, inserting a small piece of paper between each of the carbon copies to prevent smudging. I passed the test but would soon wish I hadn't.

Within a week I was working as a secretary for an engineering company only ten minutes' walk from our flat. The pay was better, but not much, about $55 a week, but it was an increase and I could walk to work. I couldn't wait to tell Clive when he came home.

Things were looking good for us financially, but getting around was becoming a problem. We couldn't go very far without transport, so the next thing we needed was a driving licence. Neither of us had one. Having been at sea for ten years, Clive had never driven a car. There was no reason to. And my Burmese licence would definitely not be acceptable. So we'd have to take driving lessons. Me first, as I'd been driving for a while, in a fashion. I just had to get used to giving way to the right. Melbourne traffic terrified me. For two years I'd been driving around Rangoon where cars were almost non-existent. Just a few little three-wheeled tuk-tuks and one or two taxis. The more modern vehicles had belonged to foreigners like me, mainly from overseas Embassies. Now I would be driving in real traffic. It was a bit scary.

After five lessons, learning how to cope with trams, three-lane traffic and nose to nose right turns, my instructor decided I was ready to take the test. I still wasn't confident, but I managed to pass and soon we were on a train to Geelong to buy our first car. It was also our first train journey in Australia and it was quite an experience, one we can both still vividly recall. We had a first-class compartment to ourselves, with long leather seats on each side and luggage racks above our heads, but we were freezing and there didn't appear to be any heating. As we were searching for a switch of some kind, the door opened and what looked like a big lump of hot tar was thrown into the carriage.

"What's that?" I yelled, jumping back from the door.

No answer. There wasn't one really. Neither of us knew what it was, but we knew it was there for a purpose. To heat the carriage. After staring at it for some time, Clive decided it was a kerosene tin, filled with hot tar. So we put our feet on it. I can't say that it kept us warm for the rest of the journey, but it took the chill off a bit. I guess the heating facilities in Melbourne trains will have improved by now.

We had chosen a gold Toyota Corolla. It was my job to drive it back to Melbourne and I wasn't looking forward to that journey. As we approached the city I was petrified as I steered my way cautiously through unfamiliar territory, eyes glued to the road, while my husband sat contentedly in the passenger seat, pointing out the road signs. But we made it safely and we had transport at last.

Clive was so happy to have a car but he wasn't a driver yet.

"Let's go for a drive," he'd say.

"Where to?"

"Oh, just up the road."

I thought he was crazy. Who would want to go out at night driving around aimlessly? It was bad enough during the day. Every Monday morning on the way to work, we'd see broken glass and other debris at some intersections, from collisions that had happened over the weekend.

"More victims of the give way to right rule," I'd remark to emphasise my opposition to driving anywhere unless I had to.

However, as soon as he got his licence a couple of months later, we made a few voyages of discovery into the surrounding suburbs, at night, without any ill effects.

★★★

I worked with some very friendly people, but there always seemed to be an undercurrent of resentment from a few other members of staff. This attitude, which I was to encounter many times, created a barrier to spontaneous conversation. And it affected me socially, as I was never willing to express an opinion until I knew someone well enough to anticipate the likely response. My lively and outgoing personality was being smothered in mixed company so I was quite happy to socialise with other POMs, an acronym for Prisoner of Mother England, which is often said in quite a friendly way, but I objected to being called a pommy bastard even in a joking manner.

The question I always feared most was: "And what do you think of Australia?"

How do you say the right thing? It was very difficult to give a positive answer when inside I was crying 'I want to go home!' Not very mature, but that was how I felt at that time. I always tried not to be a 'whinging pom' which wasn't a very fair description of British migrants anyway. It's not that they don't like Australia, they're just homesick for the familiar, even if it's only pork pies, mushy peas, and Coronation Street. And we Poms had to be very careful not to mention the word 'home' when talking about England. That was definitely a dirty word, which usually brought forth a number of quite hurtful responses.

"Why don't you just go back there?"

"What's so bloody good about England anyway? It's always

raining."

"The beer's warm."

"It's overcrowded."

It all took a bit of getting used to after living in a closed community in Burma, where everyone pined for familiar tastes and places and the Burmese people never asked how we liked living there.

June heralds the end of the financial year in Australia and, as I was working for the accountant, I was typing sheets and sheets of figures every day; on a manual typewriter with carbon copies. My boss was a stickler for punctuality and efficiency and one very wet morning, having walked to work, I arrived saturated from head to toe. I'd just taken off my shoes to dry them in front of the tiny electric heater when he came rushing through the door. The reprimand went something like this:

"What's going on here? You're dragging your feet this morning, aren't you? Now get to work. You might get away with this sort of behaviour in England but not here. This is the busiest time of the year in Australia."

Well! I'd never been spoken to like that before. I went back to my desk, seething with anger and frustration. I wanted to go into his office, tell him what I thought of him and walk out. But I didn't. Not immediately anyway. I waited until lunchtime, went home and didn't go back. I would have loved to have been a fly on the wall after lunch. The end of financial year, so much to do. What a mess! I'd never walked out of a job before and I've never done it since. But it was a great feeling. There was a downside though. I had to forfeit my pay and the employment agency who sent me to the company didn't want to know me.

But, as Australians say, 'No worries, mate.' Not for a young woman who can take shorthand at 120 wpm and type at 60 wpm. Another agency was happy to take advantage of my secretarial skills and I was soon employed again, working for the Sales Manager with a company called Nylex in Richmond. At my interview I was shown the car park by the Assistant Manager. He seemed quite surprised that I had a car.

"What make is it?"

"A Toyota Corolla."

"A new one?"

"Yes."

"You, Poms. You come over here, take our jobs, live in posh suburbs and buy new cars. I've lived here all my life and I've never been able to buy a new car."

What could I say to that? I thanked him for his help, wondering what kind of situation I had landed myself in. It wasn't unusual to be criticised for being in Australia. As a Pom, I wasn't allowed to complain. I remember a day in January. It had been raining all week and I glanced out of the window.

"Just look at the rain. It hasn't stopped all week," I remarked.

"Well, what's it like in England in January? Go back there if you don't like it here," was the response from one of my co-workers.

Looking back, it was no wonder I didn't talk much. Clive said he hadn't had any similar problems and didn't understand mine. Was this because he didn't come from England or just that he has a thicker skin? Maybe a bit of both.

At Nylex, I worked with an English lady who'd been in Australia for twenty years. She and her husband were great to talk to and we became good friends. They had five children and had lived in South Australia, New South Wales and now Victoria. They loved Australia and I welcomed the positive input from them. However, my deepening sadness didn't stem from not liking Australia, it came from a need to be with my family. I didn't expect Australia to be like England. Even if it was, I would still have been homesick.

Peter, a friend Clive had sailed with, owned a flat in Balaclava and was looking for tenants. We were happy to oblige. It was much bigger than our current abode in South Yarra, but it was unfurnished, so we had a great time wandering around second-hand furniture shops looking for something to sit and sleep on. Credit cards were a curse of the future at that time, so we had to save our dollars and cents for big purchases. But oh, the feeling when we could finally go out and buy an item we'd saved up for. Even buying an LP (long playing record for those unfamiliar with the term) was cause for celebration. Do people get that feeling in these days of instant gratification? I don't think so.

Before I joined the Diplomatic Service, I'd enrolled in a Teachers' Shorthand Diploma Course in Sunderland. I'd had to withdraw from the course when I went to London but was now keen to take it up again, so I enquired about doing something similar at South Melbourne Technical College in the evening. When the Head of Commerce called to say they didn't run the course, but I didn't need a qualification to teach typewriting in the evening and would I be interested in teaching two nights a week, I was terrified. I'd never taught anything before. I needed to be taught how to teach. I said I would call back.

One of the first things I learned about Clive was that he oozed confidence and couldn't understand people who didn't. If I said I didn't know how to get to a place, his response would be:

"Well, they all speak English here."

So, when I told him about the job offer and my doubts about accepting it, I shouldn't have been surprised at his response:

"Don't be silly. Of course you can do it. You'll be fine."

He had so much confidence, there was enough for the two of us. So that's how I started teaching, not shorthand which was the subject I'd been studying, but typewriting. And what an experience that was!

On the first night of the new term, I went straight from work in

Richmond to South Melbourne Tech, and after exploring most of the building, I eventually found the classroom. What a shock I got when I saw the typewriters. They were really old, black manuals, and the typewriter ribbons were inserted on a spool on each side of the machine. I'd never seen a typewriter as old as that. To make matters worse, there was no syllabus and no books. In fact, no materials at all except for a small amount of typing paper on the desk.

"Excuse me. Is this the beginners' typing class?"

"Yes. Yes, it is. Please take a seat."

As I turned to address the two young women standing at the door, the rest of the class arrived, a total of ten students. All women of course. I'd just started showing them how to insert a sheet of paper into their typewriters when the door opened and a group of people walked into the room. One of them, obviously a teacher, walked up to a cupboard at the back of the classroom, opened it and proceeded to distribute textbooks to the others. Students I assumed.

He must have noticed my look of confusion.

"Oh, just carry on."

"Right. OK."

No apologies or reasons for the intrusion of twenty people into my classroom on the first night of the term. And that wasn't the end of it. After this group left, there was a continuous stream of people in and out for the next two hours. I found out later that all the books for the evening classes were kept in cupboards in my classroom, and, as this was the first day of term, the books had to be distributed from there while I was teaching.

Having no textbook to work from, I had to improvise, so I picked up a ruler I happened to find in the desk drawer, along with some chalk, wrote the 'home keys' on the blackboard, asdf;lkj, and proceeded to repeat the letters while tapping them out on the board. I'm sure my first class as a typing teacher will stay forever in the memories of those students as well as my own. It was definitely remembered by the only teacher who had acknowledged my existence that evening. I was signing the attendance book a few weeks later when he recognised me.

"Oh, I remember you, you're the music teacher." Was he joking?

A change of management at Nylex prompted my decision to find another position, this time as an Administrative Assistant with Beecham Research Laboratories at their sales office in Carlton. The office was situated on the ground floor of a terraced house in Drummond Street and I was the only staff member, apart from the sales representatives who were constantly on the move. They appeared about once or twice a week to pick up supplies and drop off their reports. So I was often there alone for most of the day. Looking back, this was probably not the best type of environment for me and did little to lighten my increasing bouts of melancholy. Fridays were good when all the reps came in for the weekly meeting. It meant more work for me, but I enjoyed the company.

The job was interesting, still typing, but very different from anything I'd done before. I typed a lot of reports on the new pharmaceuticals being developed by different companies. Reading the contraindications and side effects of different medications was an eye-opener and made me very aware of the need to always read the accompanying leaflets of any medication prescribed for me or my family.

Melbourne was notorious for power cuts at that time and there were a few when I was working in Carlton, caused by striking workers, and always in winter. The government issued statements about keeping our power use to a minimum. One very cold morning I was sitting at my desk wearing a coat and scarf, my fingers so cold I could hardly type, when one of the reps – Bernie his name was – came into the office.

"It's freezing in here. Why haven't you got the heater on?"

"Well," I replied, "we've been told to keep power usage to a minimum and as a Pommy migrant, I don't want to be accused of flouting the rules by any of the other reps, should they decide to wander in today."

"Bullshit. You work here, you pay your taxes, you've as much right as anyone else to use the power."

Having said his piece, he wrote on a sheet of A4 paper 'This heater was turned on by Bernie'. Then he switched on the heater and placed the paper next to it. Silly me. Just trying to avoid altercations in my workplace.

✯✯✯

It was around this time, shortly after Clive became an Australian citizen, that I started making inquiries about a visa for him to live in England. I was becoming more and more withdrawn and moody and he reckoned we should give it a try. So, in high spirits, I went to the British Consulate to ask how I could arrange for my husband to migrate to England. The conversation will remain etched in my mind forever.

"It's not possible."

"Why not?"

"Because he's an alien."

"You talk like he's from Mars. And anyway, I'm English."

"Doesn't matter. If we let everyone in who's married to a British citizen, we'd have hundreds of people marrying just to get to the UK."

"But that means I'll never be able to live in my country again."

"You should have thought of that before you married him."

How rude and unhelpful. Now I was serving a life sentence; living in Australia, never to be released. Just like the spies who had defected to Russia. And to add to our troubles, we had to move again. Pete was no longer at sea and he and his partner, Mernda, needed their flat. So we were back to flat-hunting in Melbourne. This would be the third change of address in eighteen months. But finding a place wasn't a problem in Melbourne at that time, and very soon we moved into a newly renovated block of flats in Chapel Street, East St Kilda, not far from Balaclava.

We had settled down well in Australia. We both had jobs we liked and we had a good social life. But it wasn't enough. My depression deepened. I was becoming more withdrawn, and moody, crying without knowing why and sleeping too much or not enough. Choosing to live in Australia was one thing, but knowing that I could never live in England with my husband brought on more intense feelings of frustration and isolation.

Clive suggested I go back to England myself for a few months, but how could I? I didn't want to leave him. I might want to stay there, and what would be the point? If I was in the UK, it might be fine for a week or so but then I could be in the same situation, wanting to get back to Australia to Clive. I'd spent most of my time in Burma wanting to go home. Now I could go home, but I wanted to be with my husband. That was where my heart was, wherever he was. There is a saying about family that sums it up: *'the chain may lengthen but it never parts'*. (Homesick in Heaven, Oliver Wendell Holmes) That's how it was with me. I was so far away, being tugged in two directions. And there was a bigger emotional tug waiting just around the corner.

Mam and Dad - June 1943

Me age 5

Age 11 in Durham Chare

Bishop Auckland Girls' Grammar School

The three of us. Carol 5, Olwyn 10 and me 15.

Durham Chare. There were three houses here in 1955

Mam and me in Blackpool in 1960

Three sisters: Mam, Aunt Ruth and Aunt Agnes

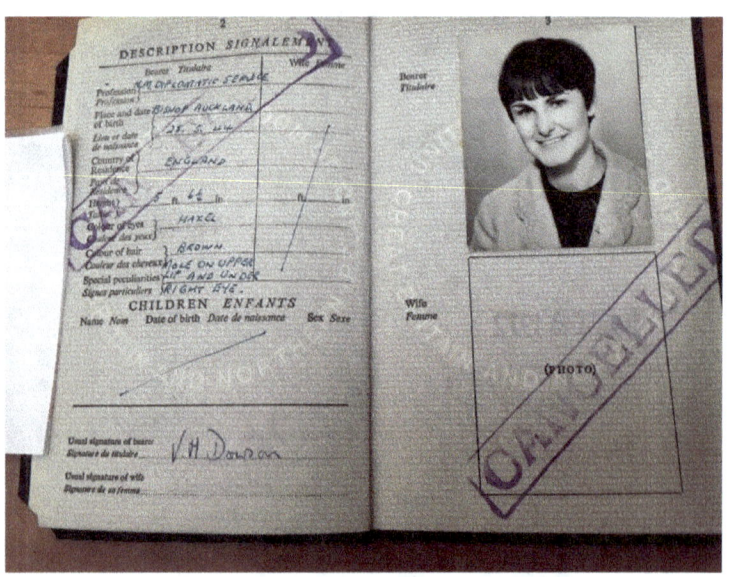

My first passport.

Ready to leave. March 1967

Burmese Driving Licence

Woodbridge House. My flat was on the ground floor.

With friends at Shwedagon Pagoda

Clive age 16

Clive's Dad 1964

Clive's Mam 1964

The Barpeta

Mam and Dad's 25th Wedding Anniversary

Engagement in Bombay - July 1968

With Liz at Hanging Gardens in Bombay

'I'm backing out' party at my flat

'I'm backing out' party at my flat

Our wedding on 18 December 1968

Our wedding reception
18 December 1968

Our wedding on 18 December 1968

Olwyn's wedding 1970

Carol's wedding 1976

Happy to be home

Happy to be home

Chase Farm Hospital, Enfield, Middlesex, June 1974

Mam, Nanna Thompson, Clive and Julianne

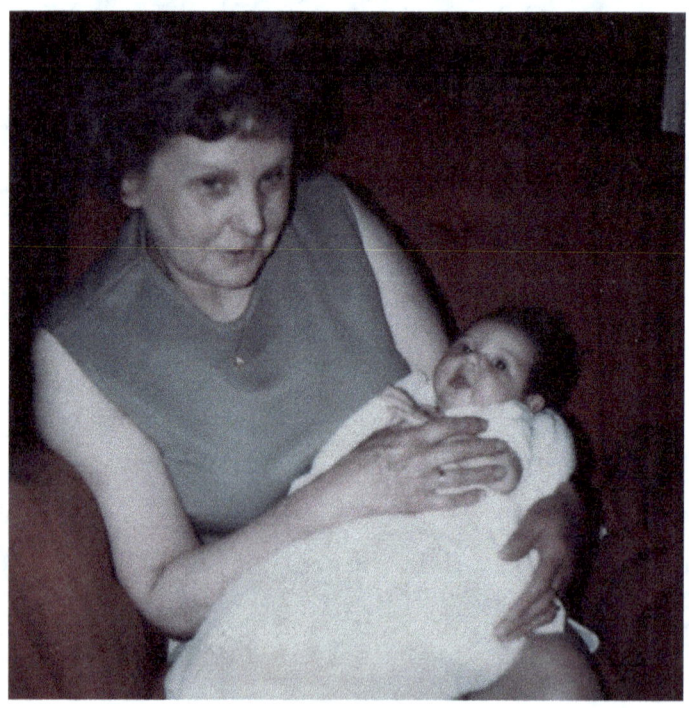

Mam with Julianne July 1974

Julianne age two in Perth 1976

Steven's Baptism April 1978

Julianne 4, Steven 7 months

Julianne on her First Communion Day

Steven with Uncle Ivan on his Confirmation Day

Steven, Head Boy in 1990

Julianne, dressed for competition

Steven ready for TBall

Mam and Dad at the Kings Head, Stanley

Doreen and Eddie's Wedding
From left back: Warren, Me, Clive, Mrs Carter, (Ivan's Mam), Doreen and Eddie, Shirley, Ivan, Brenda and Peter.
Front row left Steven, Pamela, Julianne and Granny Mac

Dad with Mohammad Ali when he visited Newcastle in 1977

Dad with Mohammad Ali in 1977

The four of us in 1992

Family visit to the UK in 1994

Family visit to the UK in 1994

Julianne and Grant's wedding in 2008

Julianne and Grant's wedding in 2008

The Proposal

The Wedding 2018

The Wedding 2018

Our Golden Wedding Anniversary 2018

17

Decision Time

Melbourne, 1970-1971

Communication – a word I'd rarely used and had never had to think about in relation to myself and the people I loved. It just happened. Now, communication between me and my family and friends was slow. Not the time it took to travel between countries, but the time between something happening and someone putting pen to paper to let me know. Even phoning was slow. There was no international direct dialling. You had to book calls through the operator and sometimes that could take a couple of days. So, when my sister Olwyn wrote to tell me she was getting married, everything was already arranged. We three sisters had always imagined we would be bridesmaids or maids of honour at each other's weddings. Well, I had made it impossible for them to be at my wedding and I certainly wasn't going to be at Olwyn's. Apart from the expense, I was too afraid that I might not want to come back.

Many years later, I would learn that Olwyn and Tim didn't want a big wedding, only a marriage. They were still at college and had decided on a registry office, but Dad had insisted that Olwyn had to have a proper wedding for Mam because I didn't get married at home. My absence had affected my family more than I had ever realised it could. I had caused problems where there should have been none. I was interfering with my sister's wedding plans and I wasn't even there.

But I was homesick and selfishly thinking only of myself and how I was hurting. The fact that the family I'd left behind were missing something too – my presence – never entered my head at that time. I remember saying to Mam that she had other daughters so she wouldn't miss me as much.

"I'll always miss you," she said, "because Olwyn and Carol aren't you. You're all my daughters and I love you all, but you're all different. Only you are you."

A bit of a strange sentence, but the meaning was obvious enough. And I missed them too, all of them. They'd never know how much. I was the eldest daughter, the big sister who had joined the Diplomatic Service, travelled overseas and was now married and happily living in Australia. But happy was not the word that could be used to describe my state of mind at that time in my life.

I'm lying on the bed. I'm crying. Again. Great, racking sobs, ripping my body apart, while my mind struggles to find a way through the thick, black cloud that's trying to suffocate me. My throat is sore. My eyes hurt. The sobs begin to subside. The fog remains. And it's getting stronger. I won't be able to hide it much longer. They'll say I need help. I don't. I know what the problem is. I know what to do. I'm just too afraid to do it. What if it doesn't work? How much longer can I pretend everything's OK?

The term "Black Dog" was used by Winston Churchill, among other well-known individuals, to describe the bouts of depression I was experiencing. And black is a good description. I had no control over the feelings of hopelessness that began to envelop me. I'd never experienced anything like it before and it was really scary. Was I on the verge of a mental breakdown? Once it happened would it mend? Could I come back from this? Looking back and asking how I'd arrived at this miserable place in my life was not helping. I knew how I came to be there. I just didn't know how to leave. I finally took Clive's advice and went to see a doctor.

Doctor Love's surgery was on the ground floor of our block of flats. Not far in physical distance but an extremely long way from where I was in my head, and where I needed to be. What would I say to him? How could I explain? I hadn't put it into words before. Not even Clive knew the extent of my torment. Would Doctor Love think I was mad?

"Mrs McCabe? You can go in now."

I walked timidly into his surgery, not knowing how I would describe what was happening to me.

"Please sit down. How can I help you today?"

Suddenly, I was talking. Like a river in full flood, the words came rushing from my mouth and I was pouring my heart out to this stranger. He listened patiently to my descriptions of black moods, frustration, loneliness, anger, resentment, loss of appetite and sleeplessness, writing notes on his notepad and asking the occasional question.

Then, out of the blue: "Have you ever thought of taking your own life?"

I was shocked. I would never do such a thing. Would I? Dr Love obviously perceived something in me, and I was not about to go there. I started to withdraw as soon as he mentioned seeing a psychiatrist, but before I could leave the room, he stopped me.

"Let me write you a prescription. This is Librium. It's an anti-depressant. It will help lift the black mood. And this is Mogadon. It's a sleeping tablet. It will get you through the nights. But please think about a psychiatrist. Talking to someone will help."

He was right, talking to him had helped to relieve some of the stress I'd been holding inside for a long time. But I didn't want to make it official. I didn't want to admit that I had a problem. I knew what was causing the depression and what would help, and it certainly wasn't a psychiatrist. I didn't need someone to tell me why

I was depressed. I could solve the problem by going home. But would I want to come back? That was the question that kept bothering me and one that I couldn't answer in my current condition.

The pills certainly reduced the moods, but I went through the days and weeks in a sort of haze. When I showed my medication to my boss at Beecham Pharmaceuticals, he looked at the dosage and remarked that he was amazed I was still walking around.

Being alone all day in an office was not good for someone who was suffering from depression. Maybe I would have been better off with other people around. I'd always been an outgoing person who loved socialising and, in normal circumstances, I would have been thoroughly bored at work, on my own with nothing much to do most of the time. But my personality was changing. Some days I would stare at myself in the mirror, looking for the girl I'd once been. Where was she now? Would I ever see her again?

The medication just keeps me moving slowly through the days. I can't continue like this. I hate pills. I hate that I have to take antidepressants to survive, to live my life. There has to be another way. I've got to make a decision. Can I get better if I stay in Australia? How can I go home if I can't take Clive with me? Which path should I take? I have to do something. I have to make the decision and get on with my life.

Six months after my first visit, I decided to have another attempt at getting through to the people at the British Consulate. After all, I'd worked for the British Foreign Office, that must count for something, I thought. Besides, a whole lot of people were getting into the UK, why couldn't Clive?

This time, there was a new consular clerk at the desk and, after mentioning that I'd worked in the British Embassy in Rangoon, we discussed the benefits and drawbacks of overseas postings. It was an interesting chat, and then I popped the question of Clive living in the UK.

I thought he'd just be a bit more understanding and offer to look into the problem for me. So, I was quite surprised when he asked, "Have you tried the hardship clause?"

"What's that?"

"It's when having to live permanently overseas is causing hardship to you, either financially or emotionally, or affecting your health."

I couldn't believe it. Why hadn't the other fellow given me this information? These days, we could find the information on the internet but then you were at the mercy of the people you spoke to.

I told him about the medication I was on.

"Bring me a letter from your doctor explaining the problem. I'll take it from there."

Wonderful. I was walking on air when I left the building, there was hope at last. Maybe my depression was a good thing. It might help to get us a visa for Clive.

Dr Love was happy to give me a letter and delighted to see me in a happier mood than the last time I'd been in his surgery. I took it to my new friend and left it with him. Shortly afterward, we were summoned to the Consulate to complete a visa application and surrender our passports. They were returned within days, Clive's with a visa stamp and the words "accompanying wife". It was done so quickly. And we'd waited so long.

Martin Luther King once said: 'Darkness cannot drive out darkness, only light can do that.' I had my light. Now, I had something to strive for. I was going home with my husband. No more Librium. No more Mogadon. I was the nearest I'd been to being content and cheerful since we'd arrived in Australia. The black cloud had receded and I was looking forward to the future.

Six months later, in September 1971, we were boarding a plane to Perth, Western Australia, to see Clive's family, before embarking on the final journey home. I was ecstatic, but it was so sad to be leaving our friends. Some had difficulty understanding my need to go home, and some had already done the 'ping-pong pom' thing, the phrase now given to British migrants who arrive, leave and return. But that idea was not on my 'to do' list. I certainly didn't have any plans to return. So, after surviving another 'I'm backing out' party, an all-day open-house which left us exhausted, both physically and emotionally, we were pleased to get to the airport and feel the fatigue drain away.

Seeing Clive's family again was another bitter-sweet experience. They were understandably saddened to see us leave. Even though we'd been living on the other side of Australia, we were still in the same country. But we all wanted the same thing; to be part of a family which was whole, with all the jigsaw pieces in place. With Clive in England, one of their pieces would be missing, while for my family, the jigsaw would soon be complete again. So it was with a sense of relief that I finally walked into the international departure lounge at Perth airport. With all the farewells over, we could relax and savour, for me, that wonderful feeling of going home. And for Clive, the return of the woman he'd married.

18

Home at Last

England – 1971-1974

Ongar, a town 34 km from London with a population of around 6,000. I'd never heard of Ongar, but I would never forget it. Here was I, desperate to get off the plane and hug my parents, when the captain informed us that we'd be circling Ongar for a while. The while became almost an hour. Looking out of the window, I could see a plane a short distance below us. Then another. Apparently, only two of twenty waiting to land at Heathrow Airport. Amazing! Since that day I've had nothing but admiration for the people who sit in front of their little screens, making sure that hundreds of planes arriving at Heathrow every hour, manage to land safely with their precious cargo.

I thought my heart would explode as the plane began its descent and I burst into tears as it touched the tarmac. I was shaking as we presented our passports and almost hysterical when Clive was escorted to an interview room. What was happening? Would they send him home? What was the problem? Horrible thoughts ran through my head as I waited nervously for an answer. Finally, he emerged smiling, and we were allowed to continue our walk to freedom. My family were finally going to meet the man I'd married nearly three years ago.

I was home. The rush of relief that hit me as we walked through the arrival doors was indescribable. It was like an enormous weight had been lifted from my shoulders, and the stone which had deposited itself inside my chest almost two years earlier, crumbled to dust and was washed away by my tears of joy and happiness. I was as light as a feather. Home at last, where I could complain about the weather without fear of criticism. In fact, most people would agree with me. Most importantly, I could never be told to go home.

My first reaction on seeing my parents was that they looked so much older than when I'd left them three years earlier, and once again I breathed a sigh of relief that I was home. To be around when my family needed me and when I needed them.

I was fascinated by our surroundings as we drove north through towns and villages. The Australian landscape has its own special beauty, but I hadn't realised that I'd missed the English countryside so much. Both Clive and I kept commenting on the many shades of green, as I relaxed into the familiar, but almost forgotten, environment. I knew I'd missed my family, but I'd also missed the trees, the flowers, the amazing scenery. It was September, the sun was shining and the leaves were just starting to turn. England was welcoming us with a wonderful display of colour. I'd been told so many times that England was overcrowded, that I'd begun to think the native landscape must have disappeared. But there it was, just as I remembered it. My heart had come home in more ways than one.

Clive was welcomed with open arms and I couldn't help thinking of my younger days living in a Protestant community in the North of England. Catholicism was a religion we didn't understand. Catholics didn't worship God, they prayed to the Virgin Mary. They pierced the ears of their children. Now, here I was, coming home, married to a Catholic and with pierced ears. And my husband was a foreigner, an unusual sight in Stanley. There was one particular incident I'll always remember. Clive was outside the pub, the King's

Head, washing Dad's car. It was a warm September day and he had a handkerchief tied around his head to catch the perspiration.

"You got Pakistanis working for you now, Sid?" asked one of the customers.

"Mind your manners there, lad. That's my son-in-law, Clive, and he's not a Pakistani, he's from India."

The landlord had spoken. No more to be said. Thanks, Dad.

Clive had no wish to live in the North. He wanted to be in London. My real desire, now I was home, was to live somewhere in the north-east so I would be a part of my family again, able to visit regularly. But, if London would keep Clive happy, then that was fine. I was happy just to be in England. So, two weeks after arriving home, we went south to stay with my Aunt and Uncle in Iver Heath while we prepared ourselves for our future together in England.

I'd never lived in the south before, only in London for a short time when I first left home, so I had no idea of where we should settle. First, Clive had to find a job so we could decide on the most convenient area for transport. Within a month of arriving in England, he was taken on at Overseas Containers in London through the recommendation of his boss in Melbourne, and I was doing temporary work with an employment agency.

We were waiting for our car to arrive with the rest of our effects, so temping meant getting public transport to different places every other week, something I hadn't done for a while. I'd always driven to work in Melbourne. However, I was regaining my confidence and, whereas in Melbourne, strange as it may seem, I'd always been worried about finding my way around on public transport, here in England I had no problem getting to unfamiliar places on trains and buses. I wasn't aware then that the feeling of belonging somewhere is one of the basic human needs. I never felt I belonged in Melbourne.

Sadly, Nana Dowson, Dad's Mam, died shortly after our return, in December, and I rushed back to the North for the funeral. It was obviously a very sombre occasion but it was good to be able to grieve with Dad and other members of the family I hadn't seen for a number of years. Dad took a wrong turn on the way to the funeral in Darlington, so we were a bit late arriving at the church. I was so proud to be by his side as we walked down the aisle towards the rest of the family. It brought back memories of the last time I'd walked down the aisle without him, thousands of miles away. Clive was still in London, but he joined me on the 23rd to spend our first Christmas together with my family and to celebrate a belated third wedding anniversary.

Our plan was to rent for a while and take our time deciding where we would eventually buy a house and settle down. At 27, my biological clock was ticking and I was eager to start a family. Our bank manager had advised us to buy rather than rent. Buy anything, he'd said. Later, we'd wish we'd taken his advice. But we had £2,000 for a deposit and the type of house we wanted was about £6-8000 in 1971. So there were no worries there. Or so we thought.

We'd been living in a flat in Melbourne, so assumed we would be able to do the same in London. To say we were a bit optimistic would be an understatement. While I was in the North at my grandmother's funeral, Clive managed to inspect a few places in the evenings, after work. They were either too expensive or uninhabitable as far as he was concerned. And the Underground was not a nice place to be after dark. Arriving in Uxbridge one night, he discovered his wallet was missing. He had no fare for the bus to Iver Heath, and no money to make a phone call. So he took a taxi, hoping my aunt and uncle would have enough cash to pay the fare. Not a nice experience for him.

We finally decided to rent a bungalow in Billericay, Essex. I got a permanent job with Yardley, starting in Bond Street, London, eventually moving to the Basildon Head Office, a short bus ride from Billericay. In the meantime, it was so great to be working in the centre of London. I was in the world again, walking down Oxford Street and taking the tube.

We took a lease for a year and, although the rent was almost my whole wage, we were happy. The house wasn't much bigger than our first flat in Melbourne; the lounge was longer and it had two bedrooms and a separate kitchen. And it had something more. To our delight, French windows at the back opened onto a small garden, and beyond that, an area of woodland, where a couple of horses would occasionally appear to accept a gift of the small apples which fell from the surrounding trees into our garden. It also came with the family pet, an enormous black and white cat called Smokey. This was 16 Beverley Rise, Billericay. Our own little paradise. For now, anyway.

Our first summer in England, and it was hot. At lunchtime, I'd sit outside with my colleagues from Yardley, or we'd pop down to the local pub. And I got sunburnt. I couldn't believe it. I'd listened for so long to people telling me that England was cold and wet that I'd forgotten that it could actually be warm too. And I was beginning to realise that I'd sabotaged myself socially by taking throw-away comments too seriously in Australia. As the fog in my head cleared, I was becoming more aware of the part I had played in my own isolation.

At home, we enjoyed sitting around in the garden with lots of visitors from the north. My family could visit and stay a few days and I was in my element. This was what I'd missed, being able to look after them in my own home. My first home in England, where I could have a cup of tea with my Mam. I was in heaven.

But life in England wasn't all good. The miner's strike in 1972 resulted in programmed power cuts over a number of weeks. At least we knew when they would happen. We were informed in advance that power could be off for six hours in the morning, afternoon or at night, so we could plan for it. In the evenings we played cards or read by candlelight. Very peaceful, although inconvenient at times.

★★★

The owners of our bungalow would be returning to England soon, so it was time to start looking for a place of our own. But we were in for a shock. A big one. House prices had doubled and some had tripled since we'd last looked at the property market. We found ourselves viewing 100-year-old houses instead of the brand new ones we'd originally envisaged when we were looking at brochures in Australia.

In England in 1972, banks and building societies wouldn't include the wife's wage when calculating the amount of money a couple could borrow. Even with £2,000 deposit, we were stuck. There was no way we could afford to buy a house at this rate. Not in the South anyway and the North was still not an option as far as my husband was concerned. The bank manager had been right. We should have listened to him.

But we were soon presented with an answer to our dilemma. I wasn't the only one with family in the UK. Clive's Aunt Nora and Uncle Dennis lived in London, and their adult children in suburbs close by. His cousin Marcelle suggested we get in touch with the London Housing Authority, which was resettling families from various areas around London to a new housing project in Cheshunt, Hertfordshire. We put in an application and, to our surprise and delight, we were accepted. We moved into a block of new terraced houses among a group of wonderful Londoners, who welcomed us into their community and made us feel instantly at home.

I'd lived in a council house for most of my life and, although it wasn't what I'd dreamed of when we returned to England, this was the next best thing to owning our own home. And we would do that one day.

Having Clive's extended family so close meant we were always involved in their family celebrations, the first being the wedding of his cousin Noel. And my first Catholic mass. It wasn't too different from the Church of England service except the communion was part of the mass and there was more kneeling.

"I haven't got the knees to be a Catholic," I whispered to Clive. "And, why do they shake hands and say, 'Pleased to meet you'?"

"It's 'Peace be with you'."

"Oh. OK."

I had to leave my job at Yardley when we moved to Hertfordshire, but I was soon working for the Department of Health and Social Security in Edmonton. I didn't last there very long. The administrative work was OK but I discovered I wasn't cut out for telling distressed mothers they couldn't have any more money to buy shoes for their children. One lady I interviewed came to the office with her five children, all under eight years, and wouldn't move. They had to get security to come and take her out of the place.

This was too emotionally draining for me, and I didn't feel qualified to deal with this type of situation. I asked to be relocated and was transferred to another department where I was responsible, along with four or five other employees, for calculating the amount of money allocated to families each fortnight. I couldn't deal with the monotony of this job either … me, who had sat in an office in Melbourne alone, doing very little all day, found this job boring. How I had changed. But it wasn't just the monotony. The casual attitude of some of my colleagues shocked me.

"Can you help me with this please?" I asked my supervisor one morning. I was holding a client's thick, tattered folder, a family with six children.

"What's the problem?"

"I'm having difficulty working out the figures. It's a bit

complicated with the casual work the parents have been doing. Could you check it with me?"

"Oh. Just put it back in the drawer and someone else can deal with it."

This file got put back in the drawer so often until eventually the family had to call to ask where their money was, and it was taken to another department to be dealt with.

So I resigned. My supervisor asked what I was looking for and when I said job satisfaction, he looked at me as if I was crazy. I'd got my motivation back. I wanted a job which required integrity and reliability, with some responsibility, where I could use my skills and my initiative.

My next job was at BOC Murex in Waltham Cross. Two secretaries in the job before me had left because they were pregnant. In those days it was OK for employers to ask if you were thinking of having a family. What could I say to that? I needed the job so I said no, which was true. Almost. Time was marching on for me. I was twenty-nine and having a family was next on my list of things to do now that I was home. But it didn't look like that was going to happen anytime soon, unless we decided to forget about buying a house. So the house was put on the back burner. For the time being at least.

Nine months later I was pregnant and they blamed the typist's chair! But everyone was great, and as I waddled through the factory like a pregnant penguin, I got wolf whistles from the guys and "Hi, love, how're you feeling," from the women.

I left there when I was six months along and the staff provided virtually everything required for a first baby. Except the furniture of course. Having a first baby at 30 was unusual in 1974 and at the hospital I was known as an elderly *primagravida*. Taking Mam's advice, and not wanting to tempt providence, I hadn't bought anything at all, so they had no problems deciding what to get. I'd really enjoyed working at BOC, and, in a way, I was sorry to leave.

But I was now embarking on the next stage of my life; becoming a mam.

So, I left work to spend three months preparing for the birth of our daughter. Of course, in those days we had no way of knowing whether it would a boy or a girl. They were happy days. I remember rolling around the floor, laughing helplessly at Clive as he tried to hang wallpaper and lay vinyl flooring for the first time in his life.

I must say, working at BOC and living in Cheshunt, being part of a community of supportive, young families, were among the happiest parts of my life on my return to England. My belonging needs were being fulfilled.

Before I left work, one of the managers had asked me if I'd like to do some typing for him at home, transcribing tapes, for which he'd pay me, of course. The tapes were recordings of psychic meetings, and every day I sat at a table in our bedroom with my trusty, portable, manual typewriter, the one that had travelled to Burma and back, listening to a medium channelling dead people.

The medium was always a lady and at the beginning of each tape would be a lesson from an Indian Chief called White Cloud. His voice came through the medium very loud and clear and definitely male. Each week I looked forward to hearing his next message about reincarnation.

He explained the phases of reincarnation, where the object of each life is to reach Nirvana. We return to earth to atone for something we did in our past lives, or to do something that will take us further towards our final goal of Nirvana. He believed that child prodigies like Mozart are merely remembering things from their past lives and that's why Mozart could compose a concerto at five years old. He said that when we wonder why little children suffer and die, this is because they've reached Nirvana in their short life on earth and have nothing else to prove. People who have committed dreadful acts in their lives may have to atone by suffering in this life or having to devote their lives to others, such as their parents or children with disabilities. Fascinating!

I've recounted this story to a few friends over the years and some of them have thanked me as it made them feel better about people in their own lives who have passed away too soon. My personal feelings are that if this belief gets you through, then that's all that matters.

But there were some other quite scary episodes on tape. The medium was from Eastern Europe and I would often hear foreign words coming through her, and sometimes screams and sounds of people trying to breathe. These, she explained, when she came out of her trance, were souls who had died in the gas chambers and she was rescuing them from the limbo to which their sudden death had sentenced them. Another session which put me off ever touching a Ouija board was with a woman who had been taken over by a Zulu warrior, and not a very nice one. According to the medium, this had happened when the woman was playing with a Ouija board. This was the most frightening of all the sessions I transcribed.

★★★

Our beautiful daughter, Julianne, was born at 9.17 pm on 21st June 1974 in Chase Farm Hospital, Enfield. And Clive got there just in time. My sister Carol had chosen that day to resign from her live-in job at a veterinary hospital in Barnet, an hour's drive away, and Clive had left my side to transport her to our home to stay with us for a while.

"It's Julianne," I said as he was escorted into the delivery room.

She had a mop of black hair and her eyes were the darkest brown I'd ever seen, almost black. She weighed 8lbs 3oz and kept the whole nursery awake all night, a nurse informed me next morning.

I couldn't take my eyes off her as she slept in her bassinette beside my bed. She wasn't asleep for long though. A nurse arrived and stuck a needle in her foot.

"Sorry, mother, but I have to do it again this afternoon."

And off she went, leaving me with a red-faced screaming baby. Before the day was out, my little angel was lying in a cot with another baby, both blindfolded and under a sun light, where they remained for three days until all signs of possible jaundice had disappeared. Feeding her with a blindfold on wasn't easy. She screamed and wouldn't feed. So I took it off. The nurses weren't happy and told me so in no uncertain terms. I responded by bursting into tears. They left me alone after that to feed my angel in peace. But I had to put the blindfold bandage on myself when we'd finished. Not as easy as it sounds.

Apart from cards and flowers from my friends and relatives, I received an enormous floral arrangement from the Psychic Group, with a card which read: Congratulations on a Midsummer's Day baby. Little did I know that for most of her life she would be celebrating her birthday on Midwinter's Day.

Naturally, the birth of our daughter brought many visitors, among them Bill and Liz, my surrogate parents at our wedding. They were living in Basingstoke, awaiting another overseas posting. We'd been married now for six years and no one had thought we'd last more than a year apparently. So Bill and Liz could pass the news on to the non-believers that we were still together and very happy, especially with the new addition to our family.

Now we had to think about the christening. As we'd discussed before our marriage, although Clive was not a practising Catholic, he still wanted our children to be brought up in the Catholic faith and I was happy with that. So we arranged to meet with the priest at the Church of the Immaculate Conception in Waltham Cross. Or the Immaculate Church of Conception as Mam and some of our other non-Catholic guests reported afterward.

It wasn't as easy as booking an appointment. The priest wouldn't allow us to have our daughter baptised unless Clive, as the Catholic, became a member of his parish and started attending mass. Naturally, he agreed to this, and the baptism was performed in front of all my family, Clive's Auntie Nora and Uncle Dennis and their families and our friends. It was beautiful. It was how it was supposed to be; surrounded by family and friends at a family occasion.

But cracks were beginning to show in my ideal world and this would be the first and last family celebration, where all my loved ones were present to celebrate with us, or we with them.

19

The Summer of Our Discontent

England, 1974-1975

Despite the joy of our daughter's arrival into our world, there was an undercurrent of unease developing between Clive and I. The elephant in the room, a topic which neither of us wanted to address.

The stress of travelling from Cheshunt to London every day was taking its toll and that, together with a change in the company structure and procedures at OCL, was making Clive nostalgic for Australia. Trying to live on one salary was also proving difficult and while I sympathised with his situation, I didn't want to talk about it. I didn't see that his problems at work could be as bad as my situation in Australia.

Things came to a head when Barry McDonald, one of Clive's work colleagues from Melbourne, paid us a visit. I knew what was coming and, sure enough, a few days after Barry left, Clive broached the subject of returning to Australia. Now we had to talk about it.

We've just got here. I can't go back. I can't live in Australia again. How can I tell Mam and Dad? How will it affect them? How can I take their granddaughter away from them? And, most importantly, how will I cope if the black cloud returns?

There are always choices to make in life. But this is a big one. Is it too big? Clive wants to go back to Australia. I don't. We've reached a crossroads and we have to decide what's best for our future and that of our daughter.

"Are you absolutely certain that this is the right thing to do now, at this time? Another two years and you'll be able to take out British Citizenship and you won't need a visa if we want to come back."

"I'm sure. I couldn't stand another two years of long journeys to work, of English winters. Just think of Australia. It has so much more to offer for us and for Julianne. And it has sunshine in December. Isn't that why you left here in the first place?"

"Being with my family is more important than the weather," I replied.

Then I looked at him and I remembered. Clive had been my sunshine at the end of my first December away from home. If he was unhappy there was no sunshine in my life.

Julianne was asleep and we were doing what we'd been doing every night for the past two weeks; comparing life in England with life in Australia. Clive had moved to England for me and now he was asking me to move back to Australia for him.

After much soul searching, after lots of sobbing and heated arguments, after many quiet discussions, we eventually decided it would be best for all of us if we returned. For me, it was a matter of Clive being miserable in England. But would I be happy in Australia? I couldn't answer that question. As for Julianne, she was only three months old, she'd be happy anywhere with her Mam and Dad. We couldn't see any way that we'd be able to buy our own home in the UK, and Clive felt that his current position at OCL in London was tenuous, to say the least. His salary would be higher in Australia, he said, and he reckoned I should be able to come home about every two years. Well, that's what he reckoned.

We agreed that Clive should leave in November and Julianne and I would spend Christmas with Mam and Dad in Stanley, returning to Australia in January. This would give him time to find accommodation for us and get settled in Melbourne. There was a job waiting for him at OCL among all his old mates. All smooth sailing for him, but not for me. Julianne was four months old when he left. She would be ten months before he saw her again.

Living in a pub with a baby was quite challenging at times. Julianne never slept during the day. People kept telling me to just put her down and let her cry, but it seemed ridiculous to me that I should leave her in her cot screaming when she was quite happy in her playpen.

Taking her for a walk in the pram was part of my daily routine and she'd doze for a while, but then wake up as soon as the pram stopped. It was also a bit tricky to get started. The stairs from the flat above the pub to the front door were quite steep, and there were about twenty of them. It wasn't practical to bring the beautiful Silver Cross pram, a present from Mam and Dad on the birth of our daughter, up and down every time I wanted to go out, so we left it at the bottom of the stairs. That was fine, but carrying Julianne down there was scary, especially if she was a bit fidgety. But it was worth it to get out of the flat and into the fresh air. Rain, snow, wind. I got a lot of exercise and saw a lot of Stanley and its surrounding countryside during my daily walks. I wanted to savour and remember it all. Who knew when, or if, I'd return?

Although Julianne was asleep by half-past six at night, she was always awake by six in the morning. She'd been diagnosed as hyperkinetic when she was three months old and apparently I was lucky that she slept through the night, as some hyperkinetic children wake every two hours until they are five years old and beyond. So, I'd change her, feed her and play with her until about half-past eight. Then I'd carry her quietly into my parents' bedroom for a little playtime with her grandparents before the start of their busy day. It was all about making memories for them. Memories of a granddaughter one of them would never see again.

★★★

When I arrived in Australia in 1969, British citizens didn't need a visa, but it was a very different story in January 1975. Australia had recently changed its immigration policy. I was now an alien, just as Clive had been when I'd asked about him coming to live in England. So, when I applied for an entry visa for my daughter and myself, I was refused. Unbelievable. It was déjà vu. Melbourne all over again.

"But my husband's an Australian citizen and we're going to join him in Melbourne."

"I'm sorry. You'll need to go through the same immigration procedures as everyone else."

I was devastated. It was now three months since Clive had left and naturally, I was missing him. Once again, where I was and where I wanted to be were not the same place. Was I going to spend the rest of my life wanting and waiting to be somewhere else?

I started making arrangements to apply for immigration, and the first thing I was asked to do was attend an interview in Edinburgh, Scotland. The Newcastle branch was much closer but was closing down in February and fully booked until then. Going to Edinburgh meant I would have to stay overnight. It was too far to travel both ways in one day and I'd have to take my seven-month-old daughter with me.

My parents were busy with the pub and everything that entailed. My sisters were busy with their lives. There was really nobody to talk to about how I was feeling. I had a husband and a gorgeous baby. What more could I want? Friends would have been nice. I had none in the northeast, I'd been away so long. But, this time I wasn't going to be a victim. I had to make something happen. And quickly.

The Australian High Commission was my first target. I rang them four times, hoping I would be able to speak to someone who could make sense of this whole nightmare, but I could never get further than the person who answered the phone. And it was always the same answer, said in different ways.

"Sorry, you are only one of many."

"There are procedures for immigration."

"You have to go through the proper channels."

I'd heard that somewhere before. When I was 16. I was nearly 31 now. Fifteen years ago I'd known what I wanted and did what I had to do to get it. But what did I need to do now to get back to Australia?

Clive was talking to immigration officials in Melbourne but having no luck there either. I'd been praying at bedtime since childhood, kneeling beside my bed while Mam or Dad listened, but I'd never before prayed for myself, it was always to keep other people safe. Somehow it seemed wrong to ask God to do something for me. But now I prayed. Please God get me back to Clive in Australia. We need to be a family again. Six months ago Australia was the last place I'd wanted to be. Now I couldn't wait to get back there.

Finally, I wrote a very emotional and appealing letter to the Australian High Commission, explaining my situation and how being apart from my husband was causing emotional and financial hardship for both of us. A hardship clause got us to England, maybe it would get me back to Australia. I could only hope that my letter would be read and not consigned to a pending tray. It wasn't just a letter. It was a love story.

Three days after I posted the letter, I received a phone call from someone at Australia House. On a Saturday. Definitely not any of the people I'd already spoken to. He apologised for the trouble I'd been through and asked me to send my passport and a letter from my doctor, stating that my daughter was healthy, and he would arrange for the necessary papers. Of course, I had to argue.

"But what if she's not healthy? What then? Her Dad is still

Australian. Doesn't she have the right to be with him?"

"But she is healthy, isn't she?"

"Yes, but..."

"Then don't make waves, just get the letter and send it to me personally."

So I did, and within a week, I had a visa for myself and Julianne. Whew! Why didn't I do that in the first place? I had needed a letter to say I was ill to get us back to England and now I needed a letter to say my daughter was healthy to get us back to Australia. Another letter, another visa, another country. When would I be home?

20

On Our Way

Stanley-Melbourne 1975

I started packing. Again.

As I was getting ready to leave the Kings Head, interesting and exciting things were beginning to happen for Dad. He was a great darts fan, at one time Secretary of the British Darts Organisation, and was often asked to call the scores at the annual competitions. As in most British pubs, darts competitions were held regularly between local teams and, early in 1975, as if he didn't have enough to do, he put a proposal to Tyne Tees Television to have a darts show filmed in pubs around the North East. They thought it was a great idea, and when the first television cameras were setting up in the Kings Head, I was packed and ready to go. I was going to miss all the excitement. The programme was called Double Top, with Dad as the presenter, and ran for a few years. Sadly, I didn't see any of the shows, but I would later meet a number of people in Australia who had.

This was a very distressing and emotional parting. The worst yet.

Mam travelled down to London with me. Dad said goodbye at Newcastle station. I can still see him with Julianne in his arms. She, in her pink coat and bonnet, he with one arm around me. My head on his shoulder, my cheek against his tweed jacket, savouring the smell of him. The smell of tweed and smoke. The smell of Dad.

"Bye, love," he whispered as he handed her to me, and turned away to hide the tears in his eyes. Tears I'd never seen him shed before. I'd made my Dad cry. Something I'll never forget.

"Bye, Dad. Look after yourself and Mam. I'll be back sooner than you think."

Saying goodbye to my family this time was the most difficult thing I'd ever had to do. But how much harder was it for Mam at the airport? She wasn't only losing her daughter, but also her first grandchild. I was so glad she had her sister with her. Aunt Agnes and Uncle George were always there for us; for me when I was homesick in London and for Mam when I was leaving or arriving. I looked around the airport and wondered how long it would be before I would set foot in England again. How old would Julianne be? How old would I be? Fortunately, perhaps, we can never know what the future holds for us.

Flying with a baby is never easy, but it was eight in the evening when we boarded the plane so I was pretty certain she'd be asleep soon, and so would I. We'd both been awake most of the night before. I was seated in the front row of the middle section of the plane with a pull-down ledge in front of me, on which sat a brown carrycot. I remember thinking that they didn't know much about ten-month-old babies if they thought one would remain in a carrycot for any length of time unless asleep.

Once fed, Julianne settled down quickly. Good, she would sleep for at least ten hours. Or so I thought. Shortly after dinner was served, a screen above her cot lit up. It was movie time on a plane in the 1970s. I could see the colours reflecting on her face, so I tried to move the cot. Without success. Where would I put it? It wasn't allowed on the floor and the flight crew weren't too helpful.

"It's never been a problem for other parents."

Really? Maybe they just didn't complain. One hour after she'd gone to sleep Julianne was awake. And so was I. For the rest of the flight. Planes were not baby-friendly in those days. I had to eat my meals with Julianne attached to my seatbelt. Not too bad, but when I asked one of the flight attendants if she could look after her while I went to the bathroom, I was astounded by the reply.

"We're not babysitters, Madam."

So I took her with me.

I've flown to and from Australia many times over the years and flight attendants are often seen helping mothers with their babies. How things have changed.

At Kuala Lumpur, I decided to stay on board where Julianne was free to crawl up and down the aisles without bothering anyone. With me following her of course. After a couple of hours, I was beginning to wonder what was going on and how much longer it would be before we took off again for Melbourne. There was no one to ask as all the crew had left the plane. Two hours later, an announcement over the loudspeaker informed us that we may have to stay in Kuala Lumpur overnight. I was stunned. We'd already been on the ground for four hours and I didn't fancy staying overnight in a hotel with a baby. I'd just digested this news when, to my relief, a new cabin crew came on board. We'd soon be on our way to Australia. But not to Melbourne. Because of the long delay, the flight was diverting to Sydney. I was shattered.

To compensate for the inconvenience, we were all offered a free drink. Passengers had to pay for drinks in those days. So I had a scotch which mellowed me a bit. By the time we took off, it was over twenty hours since we'd left London, and I hadn't slept for thirty-two. I was exhausted and my daughter still showed no signs of sleeping. One of the flight attendants appeared with a miniature bottle of brandy and suggested that I put some in Julianne's bottle of milk. I asked an older couple sitting behind me, what they thought about putting alcohol in my baby's bottle, but they wouldn't comment. Sensible people. So I drank the brandy myself. Now I'd had two free drinks and I was feeling very relaxed.

We arrived in Sydney without any further problems and were quickly put on a plane to Melbourne. By now we were about ten hours overdue, but at last Julianne slept while I was still wide awake and excited. The worst part was over, I thought. But the universe hadn't finished with me yet.

Our flight landed in Melbourne at one o'clock in the afternoon. Clive would have been waiting at the airport since three o'clock in the morning. I virtually flew through Immigration and Customs, ready to scan the crowd as I rushed out into the arrivals area. There was no one there. There was not even one person in the Arrivals Lounge. Not one. What had happened to the other passengers? Later I realised they must have all been domestic passengers and, as I had to come through Customs, I came out of the International Arrivals. There was no one else on my flight arriving from the UK. Looking at the Arrivals Board, I saw my Qantas flight from London. It was arriving at 3 pm. Nothing to say it had been diverted to Sydney. Incredible!

I had a pushchair, a suitcase, and two carry-on bags. Nobody could tell me how to find my husband. There was no public address system, they said. Really? Eventually, a young lady from one of the car hire firms asked if I'd like to store my luggage behind her counter for a while. I am forever grateful to that young woman who probably saved me from having a nervous breakdown right there in the middle of Tullamarine airport.

It was much easier to walk around with only a pushchair. After about an hour of looking, I decided to phone Clive's workplace and spoke to Jim Mulholland, a friend of his who'd been sharing the flat with him for the past six months. He and his family had also returned to the UK, but his wife and children hadn't arrived back in

Australia yet. He knew Clive had left for the airport in the early hours of the morning, so must be somewhere around.

"Wait there," he said. "I'll come and get you."

"I'm not going anywhere," was my reply.

So I wandered around and kept looking. Then, glancing across to a seating area in the Arrivals Lounge, I noticed a young man who, from a distance, looked a lot like Clive. My heart raced and I moved quickly towards him. But then a child ran up to him and he sat down next to a young woman. My heart dropped. That couldn't be him and I started to walk away. Then, he turned around and, yes it was him. It was my husband. He was with Joanne, another friend from our first stay in Melbourne. What a relief! I just stood still until he realised it was us. Then he was running. What a big surprise for him when he saw Julianne. She was only four months old when he left; now she was ten months and a little lady with her dark, curly hair, pink coat, and red shoes.

Jim arrived just as I was retrieving my luggage. I must have thanked him a dozen times. He'd left the office, driven through the city and all the way to the airport to collect me. He'd put my mind at rest and I was so grateful to him for that.

What a journey. A baby who wouldn't sleep, an eight-hour delay in Kuala Lumpur, a flight to Sydney instead of Melbourne, followed by another flight to get us to our destination. Then a two-hour wait at Melbourne airport because there was no one to meet us when we arrived. The arrivals board had our Qantas flight from London arriving twelve hours late. No-one had been informed that we'd been put on another flight from Sydney. So Clive and friends had left the airport to have lunch, thinking that I wouldn't be arriving until three in the afternoon. Were the heavens trying to tell me something? Should I have stayed in the UK? Anyway, I was here now and looking forward to being together again; the three of us. We'd come full circle.

21

Starting Over

Melbourne, 1975-1976

Now I was home again with my husband and daughter. Home being a two-bedroom ground floor flat in Glenhuntly, thirteen thousand miles from the home I'd just left. The one where my family was still grieving over the departure of their daughter and sister, granddaughter and niece. Wondering, like me, if and when we would see each other again. For one of us that would never happen.

Clive had taken out a bank loan to pay for my airfare. We were together again and in debt. He'd bought a little yellow Mazda, but we couldn't afford a car seat for Julianne, so we didn't go anywhere for a while unless we walked. However, that didn't stop us entertaining at home and we still had friends in Melbourne. It was so good to catch up with them and share our experiences from the past three years. We'd all changed a little and, in their eyes, I was much happier. Of course I was, then, I'd just been reunited with my husband after a six-month separation.

But this time, I was alone a lot. I didn't have work to keep me busy. Not paid work anyway. In our block of eight flats, no one was home. So they were long days. Just mother and daughter. And somewhere, at the back of my mind, the black cloud waited. Determined to keep it away, I walked. I walked miles. We had no washing machine, so four times a week I'd hang a bag of washing onto the handles of Julianne's baby buggy and power walk down to the Laundromat, about thirty minutes' away. There'd always be people to talk to and other children to keep Julianne occupied, so it was never a major chore, and I was grateful for the company.

Washing done, I'd walk back to the flat, have a tea break, then we'd be off again in a different direction each day. A baby is always a good conversation starter and by the end of the first month, I'd met a lot of young mothers and senior citizens who loved to chat, and I'd learned a lot about the area in which I was now living. I was becoming part of the community, keeping Julianne entertained and getting fit at the same time.

But, once again, lack of money was a problem. I needed a job. I wrote to a couple of major companies and to the local Technical College and asked if they had child-care facilities. I was ahead of my time, there was nothing like that in 1975. But I did find a nursery close by where I could leave Julianne during the day. It looked clean, bright, and the staff seemed very friendly and experienced. So, with a heavy heart, I handed over my twelve-month old daughter to a stranger and signed on as a temporary secretary with Drake Personnel. They had my name on record, but apparently no written comments about my sudden departure from the last position they'd found for me in 1969.

My first job was a four-week assignment in a legal office in the city. When I left Julianne at the nursery on the first day she was crying, and when I picked her up she was crying. It was heartbreaking. I thought it would get better, but it didn't. The carers said she was fine during the day, and maybe she was, but I couldn't stand it. She hadn't been left with anyone else since the day she was born and she was too young to tell me what she did during the day. So, after two weeks, when she was still crying, I gave that up.

I was facing one of the many disadvantages of living away from home and raising a family, you're on your own. There's no one to call on for advice, no one to babysit until you start to make friends and create a support network for yourself. I was reminded of the African proverb: 'It takes a village to raise a child'. You don't realise that you have a village until you leave it. Where was my village now? Would I ever have one? How was I going to get a job if I couldn't leave my child in the care of someone I didn't know?

But opportunities present themselves in unexpected ways. You just have to be ready to recognise and act on them. One morning, I was having a chat and a cup of coffee with the young woman who lived next door when I happened to mention my dilemma.

"Why don't you try to get some weekend work at a hospital?"

"But I'm not a nurse."

"Nurses aren't the only people who work in hospitals."

Funny, I'd never thought of that. So, one Friday morning, armed with lots of twenty-cent pieces, I took Julianne in her baby buggy and marched off to the nearest phone box, with the intention of calling as many hospitals as I had change for. Imagine life without a mobile phone or even a home phone for that matter. I couldn't get the buggy into the phone box so I had to hold the door open with my foot, keep Julianne occupied with funny faces and stop her from standing up and falling out of the buggy while looking through the phone book and calling the hospitals. Phew! But I was determined I could manage at least half an hour.

My first calls were to hospitals in the local vicinity. Somewhere I could walk to.

"Good morning. I'm ringing to ask about vacancies for domestic staff on weekends."

"Sorry, you need to write in, with references, and we'll let you know if anything comes up."

Not very promising. Where would I get references for domestic work? I'd never done any. None that I'd been paid for anyway. Never mind, keep trying, I told myself.

I got similar answers from the next two places I tried, so without much enthusiasm, I dialled the number for Ainslie Hospital, a private hospital only a fifteen-minute walk from our flat. What a surprise. My perseverance had paid off. At last, I was in the right place at the right time. They'd just found out that their weekend pantry-maid had fallen off her horse and broken her wrist. They needed someone immediately. Could I come round straight away and talk to the Cook? Yes, if I could I bring Julianne with me. Yes, I could. So, two weeks after giving up my secretarial job, I was employed again. Maybe for just a short time, but the money was excellent and it would give Clive the opportunity to get to know his daughter better. He'd have her all weekend.

It was very strange at first. The job was quite a change from sitting in front of a typewriter. I started at half-past seven in the morning and the first task was to get the breakfast trays ready for each patient, put them on a trolley and deliver them to their rooms. After collecting the trays, I put the dirty dishes in the dishwasher and got the trays ready again for the lunchtime rush. Of course, there was a bit more to it than that. I was always kept gainfully employed helping the cook with kitchen duties, and I enjoyed the company of adults for a change.

Cook was happy with my efforts and when the pantry maid returned, I got to relieve the cleaners and the kitchen maid and anyone else who was away at the weekend. It was good to feel part of a team again. What started out as a four-week relief job lasted for almost a year. I worked weekends and public holidays and was paid time and a half and sometimes double time. I was contributing to the family budget and we were finally able to start saving.

✳✳✳

A few weeks after I started work at the hospital, Clive's Mam, Granny Mac as she was called by all her grandchildren, travelled over from Perth. Granny Mac always spoke her mind – another way of saying she was tactless in my opinion – which could be quite hurtful at times. When Clive brought her home from the train station, I had salad ready for lunch: ham, lettuce, mushrooms, tomatoes, cucumber. You know, a typical English salad.

"Do you have to eat like this now, son?" she said.

Well, that didn't get us off to a good start, especially when she made comments on other aspects of my cooking. As I was preparing a casserole one day, she told me to put some chillies in it.

"No, I don't want to put chillies in it."

"But all your food tastes the same."

I had to bite my tongue. I wanted to say "Well, if I put chillies in it, it'll taste the same as yours." But, least said, soonest mended as my dear Mam would say.

However, there was another side to Granny Mac. I'd been worried about having her around during the day when Clive was at work, but she was good company and quite funny at times. She enjoyed walking to the shops with us, and to the nearby park, where she'd push Julianne on the swings. At home, she would sit and chat with me about Clive and life in India over a cup of tea. She had a good heart, too. When Clive suggested he take her for a drive around Melbourne, she asked why Julianne and I weren't coming too. Clive told her we couldn't afford to buy a car seat.

"Well, take me to the nearest place where we can buy one."

So he did, and we were able to show her Melbourne together. Thanks, Granny Mac. Hooray, now we could visit people.

Granny Mac's visit must have left a big impression on our daughter, because, a few weeks later, while we were at the local park, Julianne stopped to watch a child playing with an older lady. The child was calling the lady Granny. Suddenly, she turned and came running over to me, "Me Ganny?" she asked, patting her chest.

I knew what she meant. My eighteen-month-old daughter wanted to know where her Granny was. She wanted her own village. And so did I.

One of my conditions before returning to Australia was that we didn't live near Clive's family. Selfish you might think, but I thought that if I didn't have my own family near me, it would be very difficult to be close to his. It would be better to have none rather than only one of us with no relatives. But, while Clive had agreed to this, it was a condition that I was unable to keep myself.

Watching Julianne watching other children with their grandmothers, brought home to me that this was her life as well as mine. Could I deprive her of her extended family just because I'd chosen to live away from mine? She had an aunt and uncle and cousins in Australia. She'd never get to know them properly if we stayed in Melbourne, so I broached the subject of moving to Perth where she at least had some relatives. And then, six months later, we were off again. We just had to decide how to get our car, our effects and ourselves across the Nullarbor.

22

Darkness and Light

Perth, 1976-1980

Travelling for three days by car with a two-year-old didn't instill me with enthusiasm. It would be far too long a journey for a child, but it seemed the best way to get the car to our new home. We finally agreed that Julianne and I would fly, and Clive would drive across the Nullarbor with a friend who was happy to take advantage of this cheaper alternative to visit the West. It was early July, and as Julianne had only just turned two at the end of June, she travelled free, but with no seat, so we flew first class, the wider seats providing more room for her to sleep. An event-free flight I'm pleased to say.

Clive's sister, Shirley, her husband Ivan, and their children, Brenda, Doreen and Warren met us at the airport at two o'clock in the morning. Not the most convenient of times for anyone, but a great way to be welcomed to Perth. Julianne was quite the little chatterbox and, as I watched her interacting with her cousins on that first day, I can remember thinking that this was right. She belonged here. These lovely people may not be my own family, but they were hers. My daughter had her village and now it was up to me to build mine. But that would be more difficult.

Doreen had given up her room for us, to share with her older sister Brenda, and I was very much aware of how difficult that must have been for both of them. Young women need their space and their independence. As a 15-year-old, I too had to give up my room to my grandmother when she was sick. There were now eight people living in this four-bedroom house. Nine when Granny Mac came home on weekends, from her job as housekeeper to a gentleman called Mr Hart.

During the day, Shirley and Ivan were at work and the children at school so, for the next three days, I kept to my walking schedule, doing what I'd done when I first arrived in Glenhuntly. I loved the West from that first day when I put Julianne in her pushchair and began to explore our new home. It was July, winter in Australia, and I was wearing a short-sleeved jumper! There was a much more countrified air here. There was also a lot of sand, and not just at the beach. The sky was a brighter blue than the one we'd left in Melbourne and there seemed to be more of it. As I walked, I could see hills in the distance, like there was something else out there. Instead of colourless high-rise buildings, most of the houses were one-storey bungalows. And we were surrounded by countryside – more in keeping with the town and country concept I was used to in England.

Every morning, with Julianne in her trusty baby buggy, we explored our immediate surroundings: the nearest park, shopping centre, bus stop, and the train station. By the time Clive arrived about three days later, I knew more about Gosnells than anyone in the family and was beginning to feel at home in this place described in information brochures as 'a city nestled in the foothills of Perth'.

Shirley and Ivan had very kindly offered to have us stay until we found accommodation, and we were determined to buy our own house as soon as possible. We'd saved $2,000 out of my weekend wages in Melbourne and, after a few days of settling in, we both began looking for employment. As usual, secretarial skills were in demand and I got the first job I applied for at the Western Australian Institute of Technology, commonly known as WAIT, now Curtin University. I'd applied for the position because I thought it would be easy to get to on public transport. It was a Technical College and it was only a twenty-minute car ride from home. It would be on a bus route, I thought. I was wrong.

"And how will you get here? Do you have a car?"

"Yes, but I'll get the bus."

"It would be a long walk from the nearest bus stop."

"But how do the students get here?"

"Mainly by car."

"Oh. OK, I'll drive here then."

I was a bit behind the times. The students I'd known could hardly afford a bike, let alone a car. Apparently, students had cars here.

My first job in Perth. Actually, it was my first full-time secretarial job in Australia since returning to the UK in 1971. What would my colleagues be like, I wondered, remembering the Pommie comments in my previous jobs in Melbourne. I was a bit apprehensive to say the least as I arrived for work on my first day.

I needn't have worried. WAIT-AID, a consulting company for WAIT, was located in a small office with a staff of four and we all worked well together. We were constantly busy. There were always deadlines to meet, the senior secretary and myself rattling away on our electric typewriters all day.

Another surprise for me, but a nice one this time, was the difference in women's pay since I'd last had a permanent secretarial job in Australia. Equality had arrived and I was earning more than twice as much as I had in Melbourne in 1971. That was progress.

Clive had answered a national advertisement in Melbourne for salespeople in Perth to promote the government's new Medibank Health Insurance System and, after an interview in Perth, he was soon employed by the Health Department. We found a child-care centre within walking distance of home. Julianne loved it. She was beginning to show her gregarious nature and was never keen to leave her new-found friends. Our niece Doreen was able to pick her up if necessary, so I was finally able to acknowledge the advantages of having some family around and my doubts were beginning to disappear.

Julianne was growing up so quickly. One day when I went to collect her from the child-care centre, the owner, Mrs Murray, approached me.

"I have something to tell you about your daughter."

"Oh, dear," I thought. "What has she done?"

Why do we always think that of our children? Why don't we think, Oh, this must be something good?

But she was smiling when she told us about that afternoon's news session. Every afternoon, children of four and above were asked if anyone had news. They were then supposed to put up their hands and be selected one by one. However, today, they were all astounded when a curly-haired two-year-old got up onto her chair and before anyone could stop her, said quickly,

"I got news. My mummy works at the Western Australian Institute of Technology."

"Well," said Mrs Murray, "some of my assistants can't get their tongues around that."

I wasn't even aware that she knew where I worked and had certainly not heard her say it.

Naturally, we were very proud of our little girl. I'm sure the time we spent alone together must have had something to do with her very sophisticated verbal skills.

Our weekends were spent looking at display homes and knowing that at last we could afford to buy one. A big difference from our last attempt to buy a house in England. Homes were a bit less expensive than those in Melbourne and we finally decided on a house and land package in Gosnells, close to Shirley and Ivan. It would take six months to build, and we agreed we'd taken advantage of the family's hospitality for long enough, and should move to a place of our own in the meantime, especially as all our effects would be arriving from Melbourne soon. So we moved into a small, semi-detached house, or duplex as they are known in Western Australia, in the nearby suburb of Thornlie until our house was built.

Things were looking good for us. Julianne was happy in daycare, we both had jobs and we were building a house of our own. What more could we ask for?

But we were becoming an extension of Clive's family, which was starting to get to me. It was one thing to belong to an extended family but quite another to become an extension of that family. I love my in-laws but I didn't always want to be part of their plans. We needed to plan our own social life, to fit in with our daughter's needs and our own, as a family. His family were free to do whatever they wanted at weekends, their children were older. It probably didn't occur to them that we had a two-year-old who needed a routine. Why should it?

Shirley, Ivan, and family had arrived in Australia from India in 1968. It must have been a major adjustment for them, as they'd had servants in India, including an Ayah, the Indian word for nanny, who helped to care for the children, and Shirley had been a stay-at-home mother. Here in Australia, she had a job and a family to look after with the help of Ivan and Granny Mac when she was home. It was definitely a big change for all of them.

But while Clive was fulfilling his belonging needs, I was feeling a sense of loss. I was alone in my head again. I was the odd one out, the only person who didn't really belong, and as the weeks passed, it seemed that I was no longer living my life. I was taking part in someone else's.

Things came to a head one very hot Sunday when we were supposed to visit a friend of the family for lunch. On the Sunday morning, there was a knock at the door. It was Ivan.

"It's too hot to take the baby out in the afternoon, so let her sleep. We'll all rest and go for dinner instead. We'll leave about five o'clock."

It was sweet of Ivan to come around. We didn't have a phone so he'd had to drive over to deliver the message. It was very considerate of them to think about Julianne's welfare, but it would have been better to have been consulted. I knew what was best for my child and this wasn't it.

After Ivan left, I made it clear to Clive that I wasn't happy.

"Clive, Julianne's bedtime is seven o'clock and I have to go to work tomorrow. I don't like being out late on Sundays. You know that."

We argued. Julianne had never slept in the afternoon since she was three months old and I didn't think she was about to do that now. She would be exhausted and cross by seven o'clock. She'd fall asleep in the car on the way home and there'd be problems settling her down for the night. Clive didn't want to upset his family. I was fuming. I put her in the pushchair and left the house.

Where can I go? Who can I talk to? Oh for my sisters or even a friend to chat with. I really need to talk to someone. I'm being smothered. I can't keep my feelings bottled up inside me like this. And I'm afraid of the cloud. Have I made the situation worse by coming to Perth? I don't want to hurt Clive's family. They are lovely people, but we need to make our own decisions. I have to take a stand for my needs as well. Something will have to change, but it's going to be a battle.

This was my first summer in the West. It was very hot and I could feel my skin starting to burn as I walked to the nearest park. No shade there. The pushchair had a canopy, but it wasn't enough. I had to go back. There was no alternative. I couldn't stay out there with my daughter in that heat.

My head was buzzing with conflicting thoughts as I made my way home. I went along with the plans for that evening, but became more determined things would have to change.

This would be the beginning of my reputation as being habitually unwell or unsociable. Occasionally, I would refuse to attend a family get-together which didn't take my family's needs into consideration and Clive would say I was sick or had a headache. He obviously didn't want to tell his family the real reason and I didn't blame him for that. But it made me wonder if it would have been such a problem with my own family. I know I would have been more in control, more free to express my opinions, say what I thought, able to compromise and have input into the decisions made for family events. I couldn't do that in these family situations. I didn't want to seem ungrateful or hurt their feelings.

But it wasn't all a conflict of wills. Building a house was so exciting, choosing the roof tiles, the brick, the bathroom fittings, and every day after work we went down to the site to see what progress had been made. It was like playing houses when we were kids; this is where the bathroom will be, this is the kitchen.

We moved in March and I left work in April. It never entered my head to continue working and keep Julianne in child-care. We'd been in Perth for only nine months and we'd finally got our own home. We couldn't afford floor coverings so we had wall-to-wall concrete for over a year, which Clive painted a couple of times before we managed to buy carpet. But it was ours, a home of our own at last, and I would now have time to make our house a home with our daughter. And we had another big decision to make. A brother or sister for Julianne. That was easy. We definitely wanted another baby.

To my delight, Mam came out to visit during the Australian summer of 1977/78 – one of the hottest summers on record when Perth sweltered through seven heatwaves. I was so excited and couldn't wait to show her our new house, with its enormous back garden. Well, it would be a garden eventually. At that time, it was mainly sand. Poor Mam. I was pregnant and we were both suffering from the heat. And we had no air-conditioning. A friend had loaned us a portable water cooler. It was supposed to blow out cool air but it didn't work well in the humid weather. Every time I passed it was like walking into a wall of water.

Of course, it was good to have Mam there, to have someone on my side, which was how I thought of my life in those days, no one on my side. I was surrounded by people every day, but in my head I was still alone. Clive had all his family but Julianne was the only person who was truly mine.

Although I would have liked her to stay a bit longer, the heat was a real problem for Mam. She decided to cut her visit short, so sadly was not around for the arrival of our second beautiful baby. Clive delivered me to the hospital the night before and left me there.

"We'll see you tomorrow morning about eight o'clock," the nurse called as he was leaving.

"Oh no. I can't be here. I'm managing a sales seminar tomorrow."

"Bugger whatever you're selling," came the reply. "Your wife and child need you here."

But it didn't work. Our darling son, Steven, came into the world at 5.13 pm on 9th March 1978. Another induced birth and Clive arrived for visiting time at eight o'clock in the evening. He was able to hold his son this time, something he'd not been allowed to do with his daughter in Chase Farm Hospital. He hadn't held Julianne until we got her home.

"Everybody's here to see you, love," Clive said as he arrived the next day.

"Really. Where?" I asked.

"Oh. They'll be here. They're just looking at our baby."

Mixed emotions. It would be so good to have Mam and Dad and my sisters here. I don't want Clive's family, I want mine. I want to show Dad that, after four girls, there is finally a boy in the family. He has a grandson.

I couldn't even see my daughter. In those days, children were not allowed in the maternity ward in Bentley Hospital. Can you believe that?

Now, I had two beautiful children and a husband who loved me. What more could I want. Our family was complete. I had two little people who belonged to me. And I had a friend.

Clive and Alan had started work at Medibank at the same time, and he and his wife, Margaret, became our first real friends in Perth. They were also from England and hadn't been in Perth very long. Margaret was pregnant when we met, and by the time Steven arrived, her daughter Natalie, was over a year old and Margaret was my closest friend.

But, the familiar feelings of melancholy were never far away and arose again after surgery to repair my prolapsed uterus. Steven was only four months old and Clive came to see me when he could, but he was looking after Julianne and a baby, who had a cold and kept him up most of the night. He did such a great job on his own, and Margaret popped around with a casserole or two, but I couldn't help thinking how much better it would have been if he'd had my family around. Someone to take Julianne or Steven for a couple of hours to give him a rest. Being on your own in a hospital bed, for ten days leaves lots of time for wallowing in self-pity.

When Steven was ten months old, I applied for a weekend position at Sunset Hospital in Dalkeith as a housemother. At least I had some experience working in a hospital this time, and to my surprise, I got the job. There were four of us employed at the same time so we all learned the ropes together. We were known as housemothers and were allocated to wards of terminally ill patients. Our job was to wash and iron the shirts and sometimes trousers, of our patients and to sew name tags onto any new clothes brought in by visitors. Not very exciting, but it was wonderful to be working once more outside of the house. I was part of a group again. I was me, Valerie, not somebody's wife or mother. And oh, the joy of being able to have a cup of tea or coffee without the distraction of children.

When I told Mam about my job, she was horrified. She'd done domestic work for most of her working life and was proud that she'd been able to give her children an education so that they would never have to 'scrub floors' as she put it.

"Mam, I'm not scrubbing floors, just washing and ironing."

"Well, that's just the same. You're a skivvy," – a north-eastern English word for a female domestic servant.

Good thing I'd never told her about cleaning toilets in the hospital in Melbourne. I can't imagine what her reaction would have been. I could never get her to understand that there is no stigma attached to domestic work in Australia. I would never have even thought of doing this kind of job in England, but Australians are lucky enough to be free of that kind of work discrimination.

And I was finally feeling free too. The journey to work each weekend was a real pleasure and travelling along Shepparton Road towards the familiar uncluttered skyline, I began to realise how much I loved this place I now called home. Driving along Riverside Drive, with the beautiful city of Perth on my right and on my left, the Swan River, right on its doorstep, always lifted my spirits. I'm not a big fan of the beach but I never got tired of watching the river and it made me happy. I was becoming me again, experiencing a feeling of exhilaration and contentment I hadn't felt for a long time.

23

The Abyss

Perth-England, 1980-1982

Monday 2nd June 1980. The day my heart broke, and I was plunged once more into the abyss. And the black cloud returned with a vengeance. It was a public holiday in Australia. I'd been at Sunset Hospital all day and we'd just sat down to dinner when the phone rang. I can still see that picture in my mind, in slow motion; all of us sitting around the table. Clive getting up to answer the phone on the wall in the kitchen. Hearing his side of the conversation.

"Hi, Alan."

Silence.

"What happened?"

Silence.

"When?"

There are two Alans in our shared family, my sister Carol's husband and Clive's cousin Alan, the one I'd met in Calcutta. Both live in the UK. I could tell it was something serious and as Clive didn't know my brother-in-law, I assumed he was talking to his cousin. But, when he hung up, the look on his face told me that this wasn't about his family. It was about mine. I started to shake.

"What's the matter?" I asked, afraid of hearing the answer.

"It's your Dad, Honey. He died an hour ago."

The shaking stopped, and I froze. This couldn't be happening.

I'd spoken to Dad only five days ago, on my birthday. I was 36 years old and he'd said I couldn't be because he was still telling everyone that he was 35. That was Dad, always the joker. But why had my brother-in-law phoned? Where were my sisters? I was now angry and crying and talking at the same time. I picked up the phone.

"I have to speak to Mam."

"No, don't do that yet. Alan says she's upset and doesn't want to speak to anyone."

"What?" I screamed.

I was furious. I wanted to know what had happened. I was so far away, my father had just died and I wasn't allowed to speak to my mother? Ignoring my husband's advice, I continued to dial. Alan answered the phone and started to tell me what had happened, but I angrily interrupted him.

"I want to speak to Mam."

He put my sister Carol on the phone, but, much as I understood her pain, I didn't want to speak to her either.

"Put Mam on Carol, please."

She did.

"Oh, love, I've been waiting for you to call."

Of course she had. She had three daughters and one was missing. She would have wanted all of us around her. I was the only one not there to support her.

Her voice calmed me and I just stood there while she went on to explain that Dad had died at ten that morning, about two hours ago. I knew she was being cared for. Olwyn and Carol were with her and one of Mam's sisters, Aunt Ruth, was on her way. Apart from Aunt Agnes in Iver Heath, Mam had two other sisters and a brother, Aunt Ruth, Aunt Jean and Uncle Sid. She was close to Aunt Ruth and would be relieved to see her.

I replaced the receiver and turned to see my children crying. Crying because their Mam was crying, and as the tears streamed down my face, as I comforted them, I grieved for the father I had lost and for my babies who would never know their grandfather and would someday experience this same loss, hopefully closer to their parents than I, as I felt myself being dragged once again into the abyss of despair.

I was absolutely devastated. My dad was only fifty-six. I hadn't seen him for five years. I'd promised him at the station when I left, I'd promised him I'd be back, but I'd thought it would be sooner. I'd been planning to visit the following year with the children. Now, my dreams of a big family reunion were shattered. A part of me had died, part of who I was. I wanted to tell him how much he had helped to shape the person I'd become. That was part of my reunion plan, to tell Mam and Dad how grateful I was for their love and support, for building the solid foundations of my life, which were now collapsing. Living my life, raising my children without them around, had opened my mind to the sacrifices they'd made and the difficulties they'd faced in their lives.

The funeral was on Friday 6th June. I so much wanted to be there, to be by Mam's side. To be with my sisters. To talk about Dad. But it was out of the question. I certainly couldn't afford to fly back.

Our friends, Marina, Steven's godmother, and Derek, invited us over on the evening of the funeral to take my mind off my family, to be with someone.

I don't want to take my mind off Dad's funeral. How could anyone suggest such a thing? This is my Dad and I want to think about him. I want to wallow in self-pity. I want to feel sorry for myself in private. I want to feel lost. I don't want to be strong just now. I'll be strong again tomorrow or the day after, or next week. I want to grieve at home. I don't want to put on a brave face. Not today. I want to be with my family.

It was so kind of our friends to think of me, and not wanting to appear ungrateful, I allowed myself to accept their offer of company for the evening. So with a great heaviness dragging at my heart, we left the children with Doreen and her then-fiancé, Eddie. I can still remember two-year-old Steven screaming blue murder when we left him, which certainly didn't help my frame of mind.

I got through each day in a daze, longing to be with my Mam, to be able to comfort her, to be able to talk about Dad with my sisters, aunts, uncles, cousins, people who knew him and who knew me. In other words, my family. Clive was the only person in Australia who had known my father. There was no one to share memories or to grieve with. Again, although I was surrounded by well-meaning friends and family, I was still alone in my head.

That Saturday, the day after the funeral, I was in the kitchen, preparing dinner. I glanced at the TV as the Lotto numbers were revealed. I seemed to be always on the brink of tears and the numbers were very blurred, but very familiar: 6, 14, 15, 21, 28, 29 – our family birthdays. We had a second division Lotto win! The only difference in numbers was Mam and Dad's Wedding Anniversary, 14. I had used Clive's birthday, 31. That was the first time I thought *Dad's here.*

That night, I awoke with a start about two o'clock. Something was touching my face. I sat up.

"Dad, what are you doing here?" Stupid question, asked in my sleepy state of confusion.

"Just wanted to let you know that I'm OK, love."

He had a reddish-blue mark down the right side of his face, like a bruise.

"What happened to your face?"

"You have two beautiful children," he whispered. Then he was gone.

Next morning, I thought it must have been a dream, but, later in the day, my daughter saw the tears in my eyes.

"Don't worry, mummy, Grandad's champion."

Where had she heard that word *champion?*

"Who told you that?" I asked.

"Grandad," she replied, skipping off to play outside.

It was an English expression and Dad's usual response when asked about his health was that he was champion. But my daughter had left England when she was ten months old and hadn't seen her Grandad since. Did my Dad come to visit that night because he knew how deeply I was hurting? I like to think so and it certainly helped. Instead of being immersed in my loss, I began to talk to him. I couldn't speak to anyone else about him so I talked to him instead. And the memories were still there: Dad singing to us; Dad standing behind the bar, chatting to the locals; Dad falling asleep in his favourite armchair.

Suddenly, the memories become too much to bear and I can't breathe. I have to keep breathing, think of something else, breathe, steady now, think of Julianne and Steven. Get outside and breathe.

My children were my release from the anguish of my memories. I filled my head with them.

Mam flew over to Australia a few months later and, recounting the events of that terrible day, she suddenly stopped talking and touched her face.

"You know, Valerie, at first I thought someone had hit him. His face was all bruised down one side."

My encounters with 'the other side' through the psychic group tapes I'd transcribed, had opened my mind about the spirit world, but I was still a bit cynical. Mam's confirmation of Dad's visit changed that. How could I have known that his face was bruised? Now, I believed there was something more. I haven't had another visit, but I still talk to him and, sometimes, when I'm feeling down, I'll hear a favourite song of his on the radio. I can hear him singing and I know he's still around.

There had been four cords tying me to England: Mam, Dad, Olwyn, and Carol. Now there were only three. One of them had been severed and returned to me. It would be wrapped around my heart forever. Like the friends who'd been helped by my stories of the teachings of Indian Chief White Cloud, I too was now able to start moving on, in the belief that Dad was still there, whether he'd come to me from the spirit world, or just from my head. As I said, whatever gets you through.

When someone dies, people don't talk to you about it, not because they don't care, but usually because they don't know what to say. It's the same when you're away from home, no one mentions it. It's like it never happened. Your life is here, in this place. The other one doesn't exist.

My Dad's just died and, apart from the usual cards and words of sympathy, it's like it never happened. No one talks about him because no one knew him. I see him, hear his songs, talk to him but it's oh so lonely. It's difficult enough losing your father in normal circumstances, but when you're thirteen thousand miles away, surrounded by people who don't know any of your family, it's almost unbearable. I look at older people and wonder why they're still alive when my dad's dead. Why do some people live to a hundred and my dad dies when he's so young?

Years later, when I completed a course in professional counselling I was particularly interested in grief counselling and the grieving process. The loss of loved ones rates close to the top of the life-stress scale and everyone needs to take time to grieve, to make their way through the grief process, in order to come to terms with the loss. Without support, the process is slowed down and the resulting emotional problems can lead to depression. Of course, I didn't know this at the time of Dad's death, but I can now understand that what I was going through was quite normal and not just to do with being away from home.

I was lucky enough to have one person in my life who helped me cope with my grief. Maxine, my colleague at Sunset Hospital, didn't know my Dad, but she was a good listener. Maxine was in her forties and, divorced, with three children, she'd had her share of family problems. As we were ironing, Maxine would listen, comment and ask questions. It was such a release for me and later, in the counselling course, I learned that listening is all most people want you to do. Ask about the person who has died, and listen, no advice or solutions needed. Just listen. This applies to many problems in our lives. Sometimes we just want people to listen. How could anyone know how I was feeling? Did anyone care? I know my in-laws and friends did, but they didn't raise the subject, probably because they didn't want to upset me, but more likely because I didn't talk about it myself. But I talked at work, and Maxine asked questions and listened.

Visiting a friend about six weeks after Dad's death, tears came into my eyes as her family sang "Happy Birthday" to her father.

"Why the tears?" he asked.

"Just missing my own Dad," I replied.

"Still? I thought you'd be over that by now."

He's obviously not had any major bereavements in his life, I thought.

A few years later, after his wife died, I asked him how he was feeling.

"Oh," he said, "I don't think you ever get over it, you just get used to it."

Very true, but I don't think he remembered our conversation ten years earlier.

Again, apart from your own family, very few people understand your feelings about any situation. They feel sorry for you but they can't empathise because they're not in that same situation. No one could reminisce with me.

Eighteen months after Dad's death and the black cloud still hovers. The intensity of my grief hasn't subsided and I'm really worried that I'm going back to the days in Melbourne. I'm still unhappy with everything and everybody and I'm so tired of having no one of my own. Clive's Mum's with him every weekend when I'm at work and she's still there when I come home. He thinks I'm rude to her and I think she's rude to me. Following Dad's death, I now have the morbid fear that Mam will die before we can meet again. I'm moody and angry a lot of the time. Can't anyone grasp how much darker my mental prison is becoming? I resent the absence of someone to share my grief with and I don't know the person I've become. I can't talk to Clive. I can't keep saying I'm depressed, homesick, lonely. What can he do? I don't even know what he can do. If I'm a stranger to myself, what am I projecting to those around me? On the outside I may appear to be a happy and contented wife and mother, but inside I'm crying. Always crying. Does anyone care?

I was living the life of a stranger, no longer a life, but an existence. I was talking, eating, sleeping, breathing the same air, but just a visitor to a world I hardly remembered. I was the Great Pretender of one of Dad's favourite songs, pretending that I was doing fine. But I wasn't.

I found a place about ten minutes' walk away from home, and when things got really, really tough, I'd leave the children with Clive and just walk out of the house to my quiet place, close my eyes and return to Burma, to India, to my husband. I remembered what it was about this man that had captured my heart, and I reflected on the good things about my life, counting my blessings my Mam would have called it. And she was right. I had a lot of things to be grateful for. This kind of meditation allowed me to carry on and be grateful for what we had together. But for how long?

It's no good. I have to get away. I have to go home to see Mam and to see that Dad isn't there anymore. But how? We can't afford the airfare. Will a couple of weeks be enough? I'm struggling with my unresolved grief and petrified that I might descend into that pit of despair again. History is repeating itself, but now I have my children to consider. I have to be strong for them. I can't leave them. The promise we made that I would go home every two years is impossible to keep. It's now five years since I left England. I need to be there, to be able to grieve with my family or I'll never be able to get myself out of the depression that threatens to engulf me once again. I can feel the panic surfacing as I keep trying to push it away. My life is breaking apart and I'm so busy trying to hold the pieces together and pushing, pushing the panic away, I have no space or time for my family. There has to be some way for me to get closure and be at peace with myself.

Then, I woke up one morning with a solution. For me, anyway. I didn't know how my husband would react to my suggestion.

We had two cars, so my idea was that I should sell my car, the Mazda, and buy one-way tickets to England for myself and the children. Julianne would go to school and Mam would look after Steven. I would get a job in England to pay for the return flights. Clive, bless him, didn't object. I was taking his children to England on a one-way ticket and he didn't object. I think he knew that if he wanted his wife back, the woman he'd married, and not this angry, unsociable person he was living with now, it was something I had to do. He also knew that I would never keep his children away from him. Which was more than I knew myself at the time. But, thankfully, my husband knew the real me.

So, November 1981 and I was once again on a plane. This time with two children, Julianne, six and Steven, three. Was I doing the right thing? I still had reservations, but I had to try. Of course, when I arrived I realised that my family wondered too. I could sense the unspoken questions. Why was I here? Was it a separation? I never thought it was. I only knew I had to be with my Mam and my sisters, to get back to my roots where everything was familiar.

Mam was living in Newton Aycliffe, on her own, but close to Olwyn and Tim. Julianne had just started school in Perth and was in Year 1, but when I enrolled her in a primary school, within walking distance of Mam's house, she was put into Year 2. Children start school earlier in England. Mam had agreed to look after Steven during the day, so I started looking for a job.

Most of the family members and friends I had spoken to, said the same thing, that it would be very difficult to find work, as there was a lot of unemployment in the area. Anyway, I had to try and I wasn't particular about what the job was, as long as I could contribute to the household expenses and save for the fare home. So, I made an appointment with the local Job Centre, was sent for an interview at a local factory and came home with a job, starting the next day. I got the first one I applied for. Good shorthand and typing skills were becoming pretty rare apparently.

Julianne walked to school on most days with the neighbours' children and Mam had Steven at home. I had just assumed that Mam would be happy to have my children. Now that I have grandchildren of my own, I realise that it was a bit of an imposition dumping a six and a three-year-old on a 60-year-old woman. But she never complained. Looking back now, I know she was still grieving herself. It was only a year since Dad's death and Mam was now living alone. As well as her husband of nearly forty years, she had lost her home and her status as landlady of The King's Head. And she was still angry with Dad. This was hard for me to comprehend at the time. I was angry too, but not with Dad. My anger was directed at myself for being so far away and, I was beginning to realise, at Clive for taking us back to Australia. I'd come home to complete my own grief process for my father and Mam hadn't yet come to terms with the loss of her husband. But we talked about him every day and that helped both of us.

Apart from reminiscing about Dad, Mam was also a good sounding board for my emotional outpourings of depression, and inability to cope with life in Australia without her. She didn't give any advice, she had the common sense to just listen and make the appropriate responses – just so I would know she'd heard. Active listening was a skill my Mam didn't have to learn.

One Saturday afternoon, Julianne and Steven were out with their Auntie Olwyn and Uncle Tim, leaving Mam and me alone for a while. We were chatting in the kitchen, when, suddenly, a familiar voice shouted "ONE HUNDRED AND TWENTY." I was a bit confused as I quickly followed Mam into the lounge, just as the TV screen changed to a dartboard.

"Was that Dad?"

"Yes, love, it was. It's a flashback to one of the World Darts finals."

We hadn't actually seen the film clip, but the sound of his voice set us off on a sentimental journey which had us both in tears throughout the rest of the afternoon.

I thought that living at home for a few months would give me the opportunity to rekindle my relationship with my sisters but, while it was good to be able to see them occasionally, it certainly didn't make up for the years we'd already lost. Carol and Olwyn were both married and had their own lives to live. There really wasn't much time to get together with us all working full-time.

Olwyn and Tim took the children out a few times and it was great to see the connection being formed between my children and my family. It definitely made them more aware that they had a grandmother and aunts and uncles in England. This connection has been there ever since and now extends to their cousins Chris and Charlotte, Carol's children. Of course, my family wanted to know why I was there with the children on a one-way ticket. Was I intending to stay in England? To be honest, I didn't know myself and there was no time for long, deep and meaningful conversations.

That trip was a turning point for me. Being with Mam, reminiscing and sharing feelings about our lives, helped to clear the negative emotions I'd been storing up for so long. I was able to look at the positive things in my life. It made me realise how much I needed to be with Clive and, to my surprise, how much I loved Australia. I'd lived there long enough to appreciate the lifestyle, especially in Perth. I didn't belong in England anymore, I belonged in Australia. That didn't mean that I wouldn't miss my family, of course, I would. But that was something I'd just have to deal with. It was time for a new beginning. It was time to be a family again, a real family. We'd been in England for three months and I'd managed to save enough for our airfares. It was time to go back to Australia. It was time to go home.

24

A New Beginning

Perth. 1982-1984

March 1982. We're back in Perth and, once again, the colours amaze me. The sky is so blue and looks so much bigger, without a cloud in sight. It's like walking into sunshine.

After all the excitement was over, we had to come down to earth and look to the future. I was thirty-six years old and Clive was forty-two. We had two children aged seven and four, and a mortgage which hadn't decreased since we'd bought our house five years before. I'd had to leave my weekend job at Sunset when I went to England, so I needed to find other employment, which would involve childcare for Steven during the day and for Julianne after school. Not something I really wanted to do, but there wasn't much hope of finding another weekend position.

Then Chris, a friend who had a son the same age as Steven, told me she had applied for a licence to become a family daycare provider. It was like a good omen that everything was going to be OK. Steven and Craig often played together, so it wasn't such a big change for him, just for me. Someone else was taking my son to Kindy and I really missed being there for him. But there was no choice. We needed two salaries.

Getting back into the full-time workforce wasn't nearly as traumatic as it would have been before I worked in England. I now knew how to use an electronic typewriter, so different from the electric ones which at least had a golf ball I could see returning to the left-hand margin when I hit the return key. The electronic typewriters had a liquid crystal display, screen where the words appeared as I was typing. When there were enough words to fill a line, the typewriter suddenly took off like a machine gun, a bit difficult to get used to, but at least I had that knowledge. Computers were not a fixture in most offices yet. But they were on their way.

I signed on with a temp agency and my first job was at a construction company in Welshpool. I'd been there for six weeks when they asked me to stay on a permanent basis. It was a good place to work, although the hours were long when there was a tender deadline. Sometimes we were there until the early hours of the morning, cutting and pasting, literally, with scissors and paste, photocopying and using white-out to remove any lines from the edges of the pasted text.

Then the computer arrived. Fascinating, but not all plain sailing for us poor typists who were expected to become computer-literate in a few hours. We were sent off to IBM for a one-day course on how to use a word processor, a computer with functions limited to the creation of documents. It would take more than a day for me to absorb the information required to use the machine effectively and efficiently.

For the first few days, every time I used it, I'd switch it off when I left in the evening and cross my fingers that the words would still be there the next morning. So many things could go wrong. One afternoon, I was merrily typing away, looking at my notebook, as good touch typists do, and occasionally glancing at the green text on a black background, when I realised that the words I was typing were replacing those already there Where had my work gone? How long had I been typing? How much had I lost?

"What's up, Val?"

My face must have registered my shock and disbelief, as one of the other secretaries approached my desk.

"My work's disappeared."

Between us, we soon found the problem. Instead of using the shift key + 8 to type an apostrophe, I'd mistakenly hit the control key which told the computer to overtype. There was no 'undo' key in those days, so I had to determine what was missing and retype. How I longed for a typewriter. I was always in control of a typewriter, but it seemed that the computer was in control of me most of the time. Hitting a wrong key used to mean correcting a letter. Now it could mean retyping a whole page.

The word processor was supposed to make things easier and faster, but because it was so easy to change things on a computer, the managers took advantage of this and, just when you thought a document was ready to go, it wasn't. There were changes to be made. This was supposed to be the age of the paperless office. In my opinion, we used more paper than we ever did before when we had to produce accurate work or type it again.

With my new secretarial job going well, I decided to enquire about Shorthand and Typewriting Teachers' Diploma Courses again and was delighted to discover that Perth Technical College offered the programmes by correspondence. This was great news and studying externally meant that I didn't have to attend classes after work. I enrolled in the Shorthand Teachers' Diploma Course and studied in the evenings after the children were in bed. As soon as I got the positive results of my exam in January 1983, I immediately sent off letters and resumes to all the business colleges in Perth and received the usual replies, saying they would keep my details on file. I enrolled in the Typewriting Teachers' course at Perth Technical College and continued working at the construction company.

A year later, in February 1984, Mam came to stay for three months. As I arrived home from work one day, she came rushing out to tell me that a Mrs Dowson had called from a business college and would I ring her straight away. The name of the Principal was

Mrs Dyson, so it was easy for Mam to get confused, as her own name was Mrs Dowson. Mrs Dyson had a job for me as a typing teacher, would I go in for an interview. Two weeks later I was a full-time teacher at Hartill Business College in Hay Street, Perth. Hooray, I had Mam with me to celebrate at an important time in my life.

With Mam around, I also felt more supported, less of an outsider. I'd become used to Granny Mac's habit of attributing everything to Clive: it was Clive's house, Clive's fridge and so on. In fact, in her eyes, everything in our house belonged to her son. I'm sure it wasn't intentional, but one day she was talking about Clive's children.

"I think our Valerie had something to do with them as well."

My quiet and reserved mother had taken a stand for me, quite loudly, I might add. That's what I mean about having someone on your side. Thanks, Mam.

As I started a new job and my teaching career began, Clive was introduced to the real estate profession. He'd found his niche. Over the next few years, he completed a Diploma in Real Estate Management, was employed as a licensee in a real estate office and was soon in demand for lecturing on the courses in real estate run by TAFE Colleges in Perth.

25

Family Business

Perth, 1982-1991

When Julianne returned to school in early 1982, preparations were underway for the children in her class to make their first Holy Communion. It was pretty clear to me, that if my children were being brought up in the Catholic religion, I needed to know as much about it as they did. I'd been raised in a Protestant family, educated in Protestant schools and regularly attended meetings with my maternal grandmother, who was a Youth Sergeant Major in the Salvation Army. What was different about Catholicism? My experience with the religion was limited. In the world of my childhood, Catholics and Protestants were totally segregated. There were Catholic schools and there were Protestant schools, and it was quite common to hear the expression 'never marry a Catholic.' Mam's sister, Aunt Jean, did just that, and was referred to in whispered discussions as having 'turned'.

The only way I could be wholly supportive of my children's spiritual upbringing was to become a Catholic myself. So, I began taking instruction with Father Prendiville, the priest at our local Church of the Most Blessed Sacrament in Gosnells. What did it matter whether I was Catholic or Church of England? We all prayed to the same God, didn't we? There were four others in the evening instruction group, all there because they were marrying Catholics. But not because they wanted to become one. They kept missing classes and two decided to withdraw. What happened to them, I wondered. Did they still get married? Did they break up? I was pretty sure I knew the reason why one didn't return.

Leaving the Church one evening, I'd just opened my car door, when *BUMP* … my boot flew open as another car reversed into the back of it. While the driver and I exchanged telephone numbers, two other members of the group managed to tie the boot down so I could drive home safely. I was safe but a bit shaken up. And even more shaken when my husband called the owner to discuss repairs.

"Hi, I'm just calling to discuss insurance details for repairs to my wife's car."

"There's no proof that my girlfriend was responsible for the damage to your car. You only have your wife's word for that. She must have done it herself and she's afraid to tell you."

And he hung up.

Good Christian values are still alive and well. But not in the carpark of the Church of the Most Blessed Sacrament in Gosnells in 1982.

However, despite the lack of enthusiasm on the part of my classmates, I still attended religiously every Tuesday evening, often alone, just Father Prendiville and me, discussing the differences between the Church of England and Catholicism.

"Protestants sing so well," said he.

"We have hymn books," said I.

Now there's a novel idea.

Instruction was supposed to take about three months. After four months I asked the question, "When do you think I'll be ready to become a Catholic? Clive's Mum is getting a bit anxious."

"She must think you're a slow learner," he laughed.

I became quite fond of Father Prendiville. He was a very holy man in my opinion.

Finally, all the boxes were ticked and I was ready for my conversion. In one Mass I received Baptism, First Communion and

Confirmation, and Clive and I renewed our marriage vows. It was a very special time, surrounded by all Clive's family. And a few months later, I was honoured to be asked to carry the gifts to the altar at my niece Doreen's marriage to Eddie.

✯✯✯

The house we had built in Eudoria Street, suited us well. We had no complaints and no plans to move anytime soon. But when one of Clive's fellow real estate reps asked us if we'd like to buy their home in Kelmscott, we saw an opportunity to increase our living space. And opportunities should never be dismissed lightly, so we did an inspection. All four of us.

The house was located on the last street at the top of Clifton Hills, and the driveway was steep, very steep. From the small hallway at the entrance, we could see a lounge/dining room on the left and the master bedroom with en suite on the right. Straight ahead was the kitchen and family room with a wood fire, which led us towards two more bedrooms, another bathroom and a laundry on the right. And outside? A swimming pool. Well, that was the clincher for the children. Ideal for a six and ten-year-old. We were all hooked. Now we had to sell our house. How would that go? It went well. Sold very quickly and the McCabes moved into 64 Ashley Drive, Clifton Hills early in 1985.

Life was good. At last we were on the right track. We had a new home, I loved teaching and Clive was studying for the Diploma in Real Estate to help further his career. We were both happy at work and the children were doing well at school.

"Mum, I don't want you and Dad to die."

"We're not going to die just yet, Julianne," I laughed.

Then I noticed what she was watching. A little girl had said exactly the same thing on an advertisement about smoking. This made me think seriously about a habit I'd had for over twenty years.

So, I stopped. I'd already done it twice before during both pregnancies but had started again within a couple of months of giving birth. Quitting slowly wasn't going to work for me. I considered myself a smokeaholic. I couldn't have just one cigarette, I'd proved that twice before. So I became a smoker who didn't smoke. It wasn't easy then, but it is now. I haven't had a cigarette since June 1988, the year I faced another major change in my life.

★★★

Hartill was one of the oldest and most prestigious Business Colleges in Perth. It had a reputation for producing top-class secretaries to fill positions in the city's leading businesses. Parents of some of Perth's well-known business people enrolled their daughters, expecting us to turn coal into diamonds. And we did, with a lot of pressure and discipline. I'd been teaching at Hartill for four years when Val Dyson, the Principal, decided to retire. One day she called me into her office.

"You know I want to retire next year, Valerie? Well, I've discussed this with the Board of Directors, and we'd like you to replace me."

What? I was speechless. There were some teachers who had been at Hartill much longer than I had. In fact, most of them had been there longer. How would I cope dealing with teachers who had taught me to teach? It was a great compliment but I wasn't sure I could do it.

"Why me?" I managed to ask.

Apparently, they'd been impressed with a report I'd submitted, outlining some ideas for possible changes to the timetabling methods and distribution of equipment at the college. A bit cheeky really but I felt so strongly about the favouritism shown towards the top class students in order for the school to perform well in external exams. I was prepared to be dismissed. And now this!

"But, I haven't had any experience running a business."

"Neither had I when I took this job. I came here as a bookkeeper. You'll learn, and I'll be here to help for a while."

I felt sick and confused and excited all at the same time.

What should I do? I was so happy in my job. I loved teaching. Why would I want to take on the running of a business college in times which I knew were changing?

"If you say no, they'll ask someone else and you'll be thinking that you could have done just as well, if not better." Clive responded to my pleas for help with the decision.

He was right. Never reject an opportunity for promotion. But there were times when I wish I had. Once again I seemed to have bypassed the proper channels and gone straight to the top. And the senior staff were not happy.

So, in August 1988, I plunged headfirst into a situation which involved skills I hadn't yet acquired. There was a lot of discord among the teachers, especially the senior teachers who didn't want to take direction from me. And who could blame them?

The most difficult part of my position as Principal was to ensure that teachers and students followed the strict rules of discipline and behaviour required by the Board of Directors. My predecessor had done an admirable job of managing the College and I certainly didn't want to lower the standards she'd set. But the staff showed their discontent repeatedly by trying my patience and questioning my methods.

One morning, I had to talk to a teacher who had been late for class a couple of times. She wasn't very happy about being reprimanded for her lateness and made it very obvious by her manner. An hour or so later, I met her in the hallway when she should have been in class and, before I could say a word, she loudly accused me of throwing tantrums.

"Can we take this into my office, please?"

"Can we take this into my office, please?" she mimicked.

Classroom doors started to open around us. Not wanting to prolong an argument in the middle of the college, I walked into my office and waited. I got an apology later in the day but it really shook me up.

My job was made even harder by the end of the first year when the Board decided to merge with another college. By the middle of the second year of my role as principal, I was making decisions about which staff members would remain when the colleges merged. Needless to say, I was not a popular person. It was so bad at times that the Chairman of the Board decided to sit in with me while I gave the news to those teachers who would be losing their jobs throughout the year. I was having my first taste of managing people.

The merger took place in 1991, the idea being that our college would still remain as Hartill but under the banner of Australian Business College. They obviously couldn't offer me a position as Principal. They already had one of those, but I was asked if I would join them as a teacher of English and Personal Development. I think they got a bit of a shock when I accepted. A principal, now a teacher. What was wrong with that, I thought? Just another opportunity. An opportunity to gain more experience in other subjects, which would prove to be very helpful in the future.

26

Phoenix Rising

Perth, 1992-2000

On a visit to England at the end of 1991, I stayed a couple of nights in a flat in Covent Garden with my sister Olwyn and her husband Tim. Olwyn was now President of NASUWT, a national teachers' union, and had business to attend to in London. It was amazing! The first time I'd been in London since I left England in 1968. It brought back memories of my first few weeks in the Foreign Office, and I made a special visit to Clive Steps, which I'd climbed every day when I was working in Whitehall, unaware of how prophetic that statue of Robert Clive would be, that I would one day meet my own Clive of India.

On the way back to the North-East, we left Olwyn in Birmingham, the Head Office of NASUWT, and Tim and I drove back together. It was a long journey and, just outside of Birmingham we were stuck in a gridlock in the middle of what is commonly known as 'spaghetti junction'. What an amazing sight. Hundreds of car lights illuminating the tangle of numerous carriageways ahead of us. We had lots of opportunity to talk, especially about work. Tim was Headmaster of a Primary School in the North-East so we had a common interest in teaching besides my sister. I surprised myself during this journey by putting into words my dream of opening a business college.

That dream was achieved early in 1992 in partnership with

Zdzisia Norton, one of the teachers who had moved with me to ABC, and who shared my frustration with the casual approach of management to the needs of our Hartill students. At the end of the first year at Australian Business College, we decided we'd had enough of teaching to the lower standards acceptable by our new employer, and having our opinions and suggestions met with responses such as:

"This isn't Hartill." Or "You're not at Hartill now."

And we found it difficult to perform within a system which adjusted the syllabus to suit teachers' abilities.

Me: "In which part of the course do we teach typing of tables?"

Typing Teacher: "Oh, we decided not to teach them because they're too tricky."

Of course they were tricky then. Typing tables on a typewriter was difficult and time-consuming, but necessary nevertheless.

I shuddered to think about how our students would cope in their future employment when asked to type a table.

"Sorry, I don't do tables."

How would that go down with an employer? I wondered.

Our dream was to open our own business college where we could maintain the standards set by Hartill. We would call it Phoenix Business College, rising from the ashes of Hartill, and design and teach our own secretarial/administrative courses. Well, that was the dream. Now we had to make it happen.

And, together, we did. We wrote a business plan, we found premises in Market City, Canning Vale, we formed a company, Diploma Enterprises Pty Limited and, with the support of our fellow directors, my husband Clive, Zdzisia's husband Rod and our good friends Tony and Freda Italiano, we got a loan from the bank to start up our business. I resigned from my job in April 1992 and worked from home to develop our secretarial courses. The board of directors met regularly to discuss our plans for marketing and advertising and we were ready to open our doors in June 1992. I can still remember waiting for our first call. And when the phone rang:

"You answer it."

"No, you."

To our surprise, we soon had eight students enrolled in our six-month secretarial certificate and our numbers grew steadily as we introduced new courses, including evenings and Saturday mornings.

Then everything changed. Another challenge to meet. To conform to the new Australian Qualifications Framework, we had to produce the syllabus for each of our courses, and they had to be accredited to local industry standards. The process involved rewriting all our resources, including creating self-paced instructions for each subject. This was competency-based learning: every student must be given the opportunity to achieve the same result but at their own pace. For the first few years, Zdzisia and I taught five days, two nights, and Saturday mornings. And in our non-teaching time, we produced the required materials.

Hard work. Yes. But we wanted to give all our students the best possible chance to achieve their potential. At Hartill, I'd been saddened by the comments made by some parents enrolling their daughters in secretarial courses.

"Her sister's at university, but this one's not academically inclined."

"Both her brothers are high achievers. She's not like them."

Did these mothers realise what they were doing to their daughters? I don't think so, but I hope we managed to build our students' self-confidence so they could be the best they could be.

It was heart-warming but also quite sad when one of our students told us she'd shown some of her friends her high marks for her secretarial subjects. Their response had been,

"Oh, so you're not dumb after all."

But it wasn't only the students who were learning at Phoenix. In 1992, I decided it was time I fulfilled one of my lifelong goals to complete a degree and I enrolled in a BA in Education Studies at

Murdoch University. Studying externally, I completed the course in 1996, and accepting my degree with my husband and children around me has been one of the highlights of my life, marred only by the absence of my loved ones in England. Thirty-six years after leaving school, I'd finally achieved what I had thought might be my impossible dream.

Now I had the studying bug and a number of incidents involving students prompted me to take on a Diploma in Professional Counselling. During our first two years of operation, there were two cases of domestic violence and four family deaths. How do you deal with this? Do you ignore the signs of domestic violence or do you ask if they need help? What do you say to a seventeen-year-old who went to work one Thursday evening and returned to find her mother had died from a brain aneurysm? How do you help an eighteen-year-old who watched her boyfriend die on the street from head injuries incurred in a fight? Or another seventeen-year-old whose young brother was killed riding his new trail bike?

But the worst and most horrendous incident we had to deal with involved a sixteen-year-old who worked part-time in the office next door to the college. I was sitting at the reception desk one afternoon when she came screaming past the window and into the office. Horrific screams which scared the life out of me. Thinking someone was chasing her, I quickly locked the door and guided her into an empty room.

"What is it? What's wrong?"

She kept pointing at the wall and I knew it was something in the office where she worked.

"He's dead, hanging," she sobbed. And the screams started again.

Finding her words hard to believe, I went to open the door to investigate. But something stopped me. I called the building security office instead. When a security guard knocked at the door, I asked him to check the office next door and explained the situation, hoping that she'd been mistaken. His face paled and he radioed for assistance.

It was true. The young man she worked for had hanged himself from the ceiling. And this sixteen-year-old had seen him. What a tragedy! And what a shocking experience for this young lady.

I was sitting in an empty classroom with my arm around my sobbing, shaking student, when a policewoman entered.

"Have you got a knife?" she asked.

"What kind of knife?"

"We need one sharp enough to cut the rope."

The screams started again.

How could anyone be so insensitive? A few minutes later, I quickly pulled down the blinds as a stretcher was pushed slowly past the window. Fortunately, all our other students were in another part of the college so were blissfully unaware of the horrors unfolding a few metres away.

I made an appointment with the student's doctor and was thankful when her sister came to pick her up. I didn't see her for a couple of weeks but she called me every night. She finally decided she was well enough to return to college, but only on the condition that I met her and took her hand past that office. We did that for a few weeks, but it was still very traumatic for her and quite distressing for most of the other students in the college. Finally, she went off to America to stay with her brother for a while to try to forget that terrible experience.

And it shouldn't have happened to her. Later we were told that the cleaner should have found the body, but he'd been running late that day. So this young woman had experienced a tragedy that would now haunt her for the rest of her life.

By the year 2000, we'd been in business for nine years and were ready for a change. It was time to move on and let someone else be responsible for paying our wages.

We were fortunate enough to find a buyer quite quickly. Zdzisia wanted a change from teaching and got a job as a Personal Assistant. My heart was still in teaching, so I enrolled in a four-week Certificate in English Language Teaching to Adults (CELTA). Now I could teach a language – my own. Although this course was just about the most stressful four weeks of my life, I've never regretted it. Teaching English to overseas students is the most rewarding job I've ever done.

I began teaching at Phoenix English Academy just one week after the conclusion of the course and two years later, completed the Diploma in English Language Teaching (DELTA). This course deepened my knowledge of language and teaching and left me with a need to learn more. So, a few months after completing DELTA, looking through a University brochure at my daughter's house, I was drawn to the English Language Teaching page. And there it was, an MA in Education Studies, TESOL (Teaching English as a Second or Other Language). That's what I would do. The courses were delivered externally from Newcastle University in New South Wales so Julianne and I enrolled with a view to eventually travelling to Newcastle to receive our degrees together.

27

Going Home

1994-1997 – Life was good. The black cloud was now a pale grey, its presence seldom felt. But life is full of ups and downs, twists and turns and once more things were about to change. There were more mountains to climb, more challenges to face.

In 1994, when Julianne was twenty and Steven sixteen, we returned to England for a family holiday. Previously, in 1991, I'd gone on my own and stayed with Mam. Looking back on that trip, she was probably suffering from the onset of dementia then, but I didn't realise it at the time, and I'd get impatient with her when she forgot things. Now she was in a nursing home and it was so sad to see and hear how much she'd deteriorated in the last three years.

"Mam's things are in the garage if you want to look through them. There might be something you'd like to keep," Olwyn called to me as she was leaving for work one morning. "There's a box and a shopping bag. You can't miss them."

So I left my family having breakfast and wandered into the garage.

What things? I imagined much more. After all, Mam was 74 years old – there must be more than this. As I look at the small box which holds her possessions, a bag of hair rollers, some photographs, some trinkets, I'm overwhelmed by memories, by sadness. And guilt. The tears start to flow uncontrollably. Is this all that's left of her life? I'll never be able to make up for the years I lost with her. Why hadn't I taken the time to talk to her before her mind got so confused? Now I'll never have the chance to have a proper conversation with her. I wasn't there when Dad died and I wasn't there to help her in the last few years. Who am I crying for? Not for Mam. I'm crying for me, for the times I've missed with her, for times that will never happen now.

"What's up, Mum?" It was Steven, closely followed by Julianne and Clive. They'd come to see what had happened to me and found me sitting on the floor, crying, beside a small box and a plastic shopping bag containing pink hair rollers.

We visited Mam in the nursing home every day while we were there and she seemed happy enough, although most of the time she was in another place in her head.

"Love your slippers, Mam."

"Yes, I got them from …" and she'd proceed to tell us a long story about where she'd been and what she'd bought, when we knew perfectly well that she hadn't been shopping for over a year and we'd given her the slippers a few days before.

But at other times, it was quite upsetting. My Mam wore nightdresses – never pyjamas – and she was so unhappy one day when she was telling us that the nurses had brought her pyjamas to wear. Olwyn had made sure they were given instructions to replace them, but it was distressing to be made aware of how important these small changes are to us all as we grow older.

Another time, we were taking her to Carol's house for dinner.

"Where am I sleeping tonight," she said.

It upset me that she might be feeling that she had no home of her own, nowhere she belonged. But for most of the time, she was content and knew we were there to see her. When we left her on our last day in England, I hugged her so hard it's a wonder her small, frail body didn't break in my arms. I didn't know if I would ever see her again. And I didn't.

When I left home, I knew I would be missed. But how much? That I didn't know. When Julianne, my first-born, left for England in December 1996, I began to understand the emotional turmoil my family had endured.

She left with the intention of staying for at least a year and had made arrangements through an agency in Fremantle. Interviews for teaching positions in the London area had been organised and she would be joining other young women from the same agency. She arrived on Boxing Day 1996. First stop Durham, to catch up with my family. Sadly, it would be a rather subdued gathering as my sister Carol's mother-in-law had passed away the week before Christmas and everyone was still trying to recover from the shock of her sudden passing. And they would soon be shaken by more shocking news.

My sister Olwyn met Julianne at Newcastle airport and drove straight to Carol's. A few minutes after they arrived the phone rang in our home in Western Australia. I answered excitedly, expecting to hear my daughter's voice telling me she'd arrived safely. But it wasn't Julianne who responded to my greeting. To my surprise it was Olwyn. My stomach dropped. What had happened to Jules?

"Mam died this morning, Valerie."

Nothing had happened to Jules, it was my Mam. Olwyn's husband Tim had delivered the news. My Mam had gone to lie down mid-morning and never woke up.

I'm going over to see her next year. She can't be dead. It's happening again. Dad died a year before I was supposed to go home. Now Mam. Another cord severed. Mam and Dad together now, entwined and wrapped around my heart forever, squeezing so tightly I can hardly breathe. I need to talk to my sisters. I need to talk to my daughter.

Suddenly, Steven and Clive were beside me.

"What's happened? What's wrong?"

I was crying so noisily they'd heard me outside.

"Is it Julianne? Is she OK?"

They were relieved that it wasn't Julianne but sad that Mam was gone. I could talk about her, that wasn't a problem, both Clive and Steven were happy to listen, but it wasn't the same as grieving and sharing memories with my sisters.

At the funeral, Julianne read out a passage I'd written.

"Missing Mam is not a new experience for me. Choosing to live my life in another country has meant missing Mam during all the major events of my adult life, but it has also meant that when we did spend time together it was real quality time and I am grateful for that time, which allowed me to tell her the special memories of my childhood. Especially, to let her know the part she played in making me the woman I am today.

Mam had never heard the words 'motivation' and 'self-esteem' but she managed to provide us with the encouragement and confidence to be the best we could be, and the only expectations we had to live up to were our own. Like most Mams, she would utter the usual words of wisdom such as "Least said, soonest mended" or "Pride comes before a fall". A very vivid memory for me is my first year at Grammar School which was particularly traumatic, and there were times when I just did not want to face the teachers. Mam gave me some advice which I still use today both in my personal and business life: If there's a problem, it will still be there tomorrow and it may be worse. Don't prolong the agony, it's better to face it now and get it over with.

Pretty simple advice, but I'm still following it. When I told Mam this a few years ago, she didn't remember saying it. Of course, she didn't, but I did and I was pleased I'd been able to tell her.

Mam lived for her home and family and, with Dad, worked very hard to provide us with the opportunity to be whatever we wanted to be. During the times she stayed with us in Australia my friends and relatives described her as a gentle, lovable lady, and that she certainly was.

Lately, as I have helped my own daughter prepare to leave home, I have realised how brave Mam was when I departed for places unknown, and how hard for her to welcome a granddaughter and then to watch us both leave again. There have been many hellos and goodbyes since then, but this is the final one. When we meet again there will be no more goodbyes. I know that because when I was a child trying to do my own hair, Mam would take the comb to it and say "Look at your hair, our Valerie. It's like Heaven, no parting there".

Mam's death on Boxing Day came one week after the death of Carol's mother-in-law. Such a lot of sadness in their home over that Christmas period. I couldn't imagine the depth of sorrow in Carol's house that day. Her children, Chris and Charlotte, had just lost a dearly loved grandmother and now they'd lost another. My sisters and I had lost our mother and my darling Jules, looking forward to hugging the grandmother she hadn't seen for two years arrived in the midst of all this grief and torment.

After the funeral, she went back to Evesham to stay with Olwyn for a while before attempting to find a job in London. Sadly, after such a distressing start to her stay in England, she found it difficult to settle and returned to Australia early in the New Year.

I got back to England in 1997 as I'd originally planned. My sisters bought my ticket with part of the insurance money Mam had left. They'd also kept her ashes so that I could be there when they were buried next to Dad. Unfortunately, Olwyn wasn't able to travel north for the burial so Carol and I drove to the cemetery together. We were escorted to a huge grassy area and shown a marker where Dad's ashes were buried. I couldn't fathom how anyone could tell where anything was in such a big area of grass like that. The cemeteries I've been to have little rose gardens with plaques. Nothing like that there. Anyway, he dug a little hole and put Mam's ashes in there and that was it. We said a silent prayer and that was all. That was all. A small box and a bag of hair rollers. And now, nothing but memories.

28

You Light Up My Life

2003-2005

Children. They enter our lives and change it forever. They fill the spaces we didn't know were empty and the time we didn't know we had. They break our sleep when they arrive and our hearts when they leave, but in between, they enrich our lives with moments of pride, overwhelming love, almost unbearable sorrow, and by just being there. Our children become the reason for our existence. But time passes and suddenly, they're at high school, then university and before we know it, they've flown the nest and you're trying to retrieve the memories of their youth. Photographs show a place and time but you can never get back the feeling and emotion of those times. Memories of school sports days, where they were both mascots for their team in Year 1; Julianne upset because she didn't win a ribbon and me comforting her, telling her it was more important to get good results in class. Her reply to that: "But, Mummy, you don't get a ribbon for being good at school work."

Here's Steven in his brown and yellow T-ball uniform, reminding me of the barbecue where he was hit in the face with a bat and rushed to Armadale Hospital. We brought him home with a few stitches in his cheek from which he still carries the scar. And here's Julianne in her marching uniform. We'd found a sport she loved. She was good at it and was soon leading her team of Midgets.

Julianne started High School in 1984, the year we moved to

Clifton Hills. We enrolled her in Kelmscott High School and she was able to walk to school with our neighbours' children. However, very soon she started showing signs of a problem with someone or something.

"Have you done your homework?" I asked.

"No point," she replied.

"Why?"

"… Teacher doesn't mark it anyway, 'cos nobody does it."

Used to seeing her in her smart St Munchins' uniform, now she'd come home with her school shirt hanging out and her shoelaces unfastened. Everyone does it, she'd said. So, one term was enough and we were lucky that there was still a place for her at Lumen Christi College for Term 2.

There was always sport in Steven's life: T-ball at primary and hockey at High School, so while I was with Julianne at marching, Clive was with Steven at hockey games. I remember getting a call at work from our doctor telling me my daughter and son were in his surgery and my son needed to go straight to St John of God Hospital to have a small operation on his finger, which had been smashed with a hockey stick the previous Saturday. A finger that had supposedly been treated and stitched up at the local hospital. He put Julianne on the phone and we arranged to meet at Victoria Park Train Station. Julianne had only had her driving licence for a week, and now she was going to drive from Maddington to Victoria Park Station. No problem, she said with the confidence of youth.

Steven was Head Boy in his last year at St Munchins, so it was no surprise when he became a Student Councillor at Lumen Christi High School and was appointed Male Executive Leader in his final year. He was very conscientious about his school work and would often give me a list of questions with answers below so that I could test him on a variety of subjects. He wasn't and still isn't, one for general chatting about school or social life, so when he did talk, I listened. One evening I was in the study, trying to complete a university assignment due in two days when he walked in and sat down.

"Mum, can I talk to you a minute?"

So I listened and the minute turned into an hour or more. He talked about his plans for the future, what subjects he should take in Year 11 to help him get into university and what career would be best: law or finance. I jokingly told him I didn't know anything about law but I did know a little about accounts.

I'd felt the pangs of loss when Julianne left for England in 1996 but she had returned to Australia, married in 2001 and was living in Perth. Now, at the end of 2003, my baby boy was about to spread his wings and fly away. Where did the years go? It seemed like only yesterday they were starting school.

On a warm September evening in September 2003, Steven and two of his friends, Craig and Terrence, set off for Europe from Perth airport. They were met at London Airport by my ever-reliable sister Olwyn, who drove them to her home in Evesham, and stayed with friends to allow them the run of the house. It was an hour's ride on the train to London where they could look for jobs. But not before experiencing the wonders of Europe on a Contiki coach tour, which seemed to involve racing from one place on their itinerary to another within a given time frame. I remember Steven recounting how they spent too much time in the Louvre and had to race across Paris in time to catch the coach to the next major attraction, carrying heavy backpacks to the consternation of bystanders, possibly fearing they were carrying bombs or running from the law.

On their return to London they rented a place in Canary Wharf and, armed with his Commerce Degree and Chartered Accountant qualification, Steven soon found employment with Baker Tilly, an accounting and advisory firm in the centre of London. By December he was settled in and we faced our first Christmas without him, and without our daughter. She had decided to visit her brother in London and they were able to share the experience of travelling to Paris via the channel tunnel.

We were looking forward to seeing Steven in August 2005 on a trip to the UK. Then 7th July happened. Bombs in London. At 8.50 am, there were explosions on three London trains, killing 39 people. An hour later 13 people were killed when a bomb went off on the upper deck of a bus in Tavistock Square. More than 700 people on their way to work were injured in the attacks. And our son was there.

We knew that Steven took the tube to the city every morning so we also knew he could have been somewhere on the underground when the bombs exploded. No news may be good news, but not when you know a loved one could be in danger. We waited anxiously, hoping for the best, but fearing the worst, knowing he would let us know if he was safe. Then, the phone call …

"Hi, Mum. I'm OK."

Oh, the relief! He was calling from work and couldn't talk long. Just long enough to let us know he was safe. He'd arrived at work earlier than the bombs but there were no trains running to get home.

During our stay with him in London, we learned that he and some friends walked home that evening, stopping at a few pubs on the way. His friend Terence worked in Canary Wharf and had to spend the night in the office with other employees as it was too far for them to walk home. They were safe and unharmed, but there were many families who would be grieving for loved ones they would never see again.

We stayed with Steven and Paul in their small flat in West Hampstead and it was comforting to see how well Steven had settled into his life in London. He had met Paul while working for Baker Tilly and, although he was now employed at another accounting firm, Deloittes, they had remained good friends.

He took a few days off to spend time with us and made every day an adventure. He would lead the way with Clive and I almost running behind him, swiping our Oyster cards as we rushed through the gates. London was much busier than when I had lived there in 1966/67.

We went shopping in Oxford and Bond streets, spent an afternoon at the Globe Theatre where *The Tempest* was playing and Steven and I had an evening together watching *The Mousetrap* in the city.

London. This was where it all began, where I had lived and worked before being posted to Burma. Great George Street, home of the Foreign Office; Clive Steps in King Charles Street; Oxford Street, where I'd shopped for clothes suitable for a hot climate and Embassy dinners; Piccadilly Circus where I'd searched for the Lost Property Office to buy a second-hand portable typewriter, a necessary item required for communication between me and my family. Only a couple of streets of the many which had become very familiar to me during my life in London. It was quite an emotional journey to be sharing this with my son nearly forty years later.

But as this journey was ending, another emotional journey was beginning.

29

Sweet and Sour

2005-2006

"I've got something to tell you but it can wait until we get home."

It was August 2005. We'd just returned from our three-week holiday in the UK, visiting Steven and my family, and were putting our suitcases into Julianne's car.

"You can't do that, Jules. Tell us now."

Julianne had been house-sitting for us while we were away. She and her husband Jamie had only recently moved into their own newly-built house, but we had dogs, Toby and Jake, at home and as she and Jamie had been having a few problems in their marriage, she'd decided to take a break. I thought I knew what was coming.

"Jamie and I have decided to separate."

Although I'd been expecting this, I was still worried about her and the problems ahead.

"It's going to be hard being on your own again, sweetheart, but you know we're here for you."

"Mum, I've been alone in my head for a long time now." It was so sad to hear her say that. But I understood perfectly. I'd felt the same way and still did at times, only mine was related to my family, not my husband.

"And there's something else. I have to have an operation. The doctor thinks I might have fibroids in my uterus."

She stayed with us for a while but wanted to be closer to Aquinas

College in Manning where she was teaching Japanese, so her cousin Warren and his wife Kellie were happy to have her with them until she found suitable accommodation. She didn't have to wait long.

Steven had bought a three-bedroom townhouse in Victoria Park before he left for England, and while he was living in London, it was being rented through an agency. Fortunately for Jules, it became vacant a few weeks later so she was able to move in there. But, she'd just got herself settled, when Steven decided to come home. Like me, he was missing his family and we were definitely missing him. Of course we were all delighted and Julianne managed to find other accommodation even closer to Aquinas so everyone was happy.

Just before the operation, she told us that she was seeing someone from school and wanted us to know just in case we bumped into him at the hospital. Just as well, or I would have been a bit surprised to see a young man carrying a bunch of flowers and nervously asking a nurse for Julianne's ward number. Grant had also just broken up with his girlfriend, so it seemed as if they were fated to find each other at the right time.

The operation went well and the courtship continued, along with the divorce proceedings and all discussions, paperwork, and tears that went with it. But finally, it was resolved and everyone was happy. For a while.

※※※

A few months later, I was walking from the bus which had just brought me, two other teachers and our students, to Lancelin, a beach resort 110 km north of Perth. My phone rang.

"Mum, they think I've got cancer."

Julianne's tearful voice stopped me in my tracks. What's that expression? I feel like I've been punched in the stomach. Yes, that's just how I felt.

It hadn't seemed very important at first, just tingling fingers.

Then a blood test, a CT (Computed Tomography) scan, and this was the result. And I was 94 km away, on a study trip with my language students. But the bus hadn't left yet.

"I'll come straight home," I said, trying to sound strong and in control.

"No, Mum," Julianne replied. "I'm going back to work now. I'll know more on Monday when I see the specialist."

"Ok. And I'm coming with you this time. No going it alone. OK?"

"OK, Mum."

The haematologist confirmed our worst fears. It was a malignant tumour, Hodgkin's Lymphoma. Apparently, if you have cancer, this is the best one to have. The tumour was wrapped around her aorta and pressing on her windpipe, which made removal out of the question. What now?

The next step was a biopsy performed by a cardiothoracic surgeon and then another CT and a PET (Positron Emission Topography) scan. The final diagnosis was Hodgkin's Lymphoma Stage 2. The treatment was six months of chemotherapy followed by five weeks of radiotherapy. No time to harvest eggs, it would take too long and was considered too dangerous to wait. Infertility was a risk that had to be taken.

We'd just come to terms with this information when another biopsy revealed that the cancer had spread to her bone marrow, it was now Stage 4.

Some people either want to or have to keep on working throughout chemotherapy. Julianne had income insurance, so she decided to take a year off and give herself the best chance to rid herself of the tumour which was invading her body. She was determined to be positive and very rarely complained, to us anyway.

But, in the midst of all this darkness, there was light. A few days before the final diagnosis, Julianne's partner, Grant, had proposed. Watching them both at the engagement party, it was obvious that they were very much in love. But, I'd seen relationships fall apart under the constant strain of chemotherapy and its side effects, as well as the ongoing worry about results of periodic PET and CT scans. As a parent, I could only hope that Grant would have the emotional and physical strength to cope with the difficult journey that lay ahead. Because sometimes, love is not enough.

They moved in together and, although she had the full support of every member of her family, it was Grant who was now her primary care-giver, and it was Grant who would have to comfort her when she was sick, remain calm when she was angry and deal with anything else that might occur during her treatment. And he did.

"Can I have the honour of cutting your hair before the chemo starts affecting it?'

Kellie, our nephew Warren's wife, was a hairdresser.

Managing Julianne's hair had been a constant challenge for me since she was a toddler. Her curly hair didn't grow down, it grew up and out, and my attempts at cutting were never very successful. After struggling with ponytails and bunches when she was ten I finally decided to let a professional have a go. He did and we came home, not with the short, curly cut we'd decided on, but with a shoulder-length, layered cut recommended by the hairdresser who thought it would be a shame to cut such beautiful hair. It looked good and was much easier to manage until it started growing again. As she got older, of course, she was able to manage it herself. Not my problem anymore.

"It looks like an explosion in a mattress factory", was how someone once described Julianne's hair. But it was the type of hairstyle that women paid to duplicate. Now this beautiful hair curled down past her shoulders and we knew she was going to lose it. Once it was gone, it might never be the same again. It would take years to grow it to the style and length it was now. But, in what had become their usual positive approach to their new circumstances,

Jules and Grant decided to have professional photographs taken, as a reminder of how they both looked when they met. If she wanted to grow it again, she would, if not, she wouldn't. Simple.

And what a difference it made to her appearance after Kellie cut it. She really suited the short style and, although she lost most of the hair on the top of her head, she always had enough left at the sides to show under the scarves she wore.

Julianne coped well with the chemotherapy. She'd been afraid of needles since she was a child when a dentist had delivered an injection into an abscess in her gum. Now, here she was, being used as a pin cushion two or three times a week. It got to the stage where her veins had collapsed so much it was difficult for the nurses to attach the drip, and painful for me to watch. Eventually a *picc (Peripherally inserted central catheter for intravenous access) line was inserted which remained in place until the treatment was complete.

After three months, we got the good news that the tumour was disappearing from her chest and from her bone marrow. At six months it was clear and she was in recession. Hooray.

But it wasn't finished yet. Now followed radiotherapy, so a mask had to be made for her to wear over her face and neck to protect them from the radiation. Five days a week for five weeks. And then it was over. Or the treatment was. It would be five years of annual scans before we would know if she was clear. But at last she was free to get on with her life.

Suddenly, it was October and the wedding was only weeks away. It would be another major event where once again toasts to absent friends would include my family. Grant's Mum, Heather, had made the bride and bridesmaids' dresses. And the wedding cake. To get an idea of what style Julianne wanted, the three of us had visited a few Bridal boutiques. She was happily parading around a small dais when one sales assistant asked,

"And what type of veil will you be wearing?"

There was a short pause before Julianne answered:

"I don't know if I'll have enough hair to wear a veil."

That brought me back to reality and it was difficult to hold back the tears as my daughter explained the reason why she probably wouldn't be wearing a veil. But she wanted to.

So, as soon as chemotherapy was completed, the question was, would her hair grow long enough to hold a veil or even just a headpiece?

It did and she looked fantastic. We could now see Julianne. The long curly hair which had framed her face for so long had gone and her beautiful eyes and bone structure were revealed. She was like a butterfly newly emerged from its chrysalis. Of course, Grant could have had something to do with that.

As you can imagine, it was a very emotional wedding. Both Julianne and Grant had started the journey with a smile and they were still smiling. They had coped with challenges which most people don't face in a lifetime, and they'd come through the ordeal with flying colours.

To our relief and delight, Noah James Haggerty entered this world in 2009 followed in 2013 by his sister Maya Sidney. We were truly blessed.

I have nothing but admiration for the doctors and nurses who helped get us through this journey, whose smiling faces helped make the trip a little easier. But they are trained to deal with cancer on a day-to-day basis. It's those who are closest to the patient, who share the journey, but not the treatment, and whose strength is tested repeatedly, who are the unsung heroes behind every cancer patient. In my daughter's case, her partner, Grant.

30

Marry Me Mel

2013-2018

"This is the girl I'm going to marry," he said.

"Very unlikely," she replied. "Mel lives in Canada."

Steven was talking to Jill, a work colleague at KPMG, the finance company where he'd been employed since he returned from England. The girl they were talking about was Jill's sister, a dancer with the Alberta Ballet in Canada.

End of story. Or not.

Steven got on with his life, girlfriends appeared, and disappeared, while we quietly wondered if he would ever find Miss Right, and Steven fielded questions from friends and relatives about when he was going to 'settle down'.

Then, two years after he'd seen a photograph of the girl of his dreams, Mel returned to Perth to join the WA Ballet Company. A date was arranged by Jill and in April 2013, he finally met the girl he was going to marry.

We knew nothing about this blooming relationship until a few months later when he brought Mel to meet us at our home in Gosnells and we learned she was a dancer with the WA Ballet.

I'd never seen a ballet before, only very short excerpts on TV where all the ballerinas wore white tutus, so I was happy to go with Steve to see my first ballet, Onegin, at His Majesty's Theatre in Perth.

I was amazed at how wrong my ideas had been. Yes, there are the classical ballets like Swan Lake, but the story being told here required not just dancing but also acting and I loved every minute of it. And Steven loved Mel. His face said it all as he sat transfixed watching the stage.

Time moved on, as it does. They arranged an overnight stay at the Crown for us to meet Mel's Mum, Jen and Stepdad Mick, who were visiting from Sydney and Mel's Dad, John, flew over a few months later. The parents had met, so what next? They moved in together and Steven was now fielding questions about when was he going to 'pop the question'. But again, time moved on.

In June 2016, they bought a house together. And still we waited.

Then, one morning, after Mel had just returned from a short ballet tour, she pulled up the blind on the kitchen window to see the words "Marry Me Mel" displayed in flowers covering the whole of the window. And a deep sigh of relief and satisfaction spread from Perth to Sydney.

After an engagement party at Hamptons City Beach, Mel and Steve finally made their vows almost a year later at St Michael the Archangel Chapel in Leederville on 7th July 2018.

The reception was held at the Boatshed Restaurant, South Perth and, with Mel's love of all things beach, they honeymooned in The Maldives. Where else?

31

Return to Sender

Perth, 2001-2004
Granny Mac

"Hi, Mum, how are you?"
"Who are you?"
"I'm your son, Clive."
"I don't know any Clive," came the response from his Mum. She was ninety-two at the time.

Granny Mac was a strong personality and she left a permanent impression on all of us. She called a spade a spade, with no consideration for the feelings of others. But we all became used to it and were often able to look at the funny side, especially as she got older when her mind would wander. There were many times when I would sit and listen to her stories about the past, about servants and children and life in India. About people and things that her children knew little or nothing about. All in her imagination they said. She died in September 2001, aged ninety-three. Hers was the first funeral I'd attended in Australia and I was part of the grieving family, something I'd not been able to experience with the deaths of my own mother and father. We talked about her easily and still do. We never talk about my parents. There are no shared memories there.

★★★

Natasha

When she was twelve years old, Natasha, our niece Doreen's daughter, was diagnosed with malignant brain tumours. This was after many visits to doctors and, finally, the Princess Margaret Children's Hospital in Perth, from where her parents had refused to move until doctors could come up with a good reason for her daughter's recurring headaches.

Natasha's favourite singer was Elvis Presley. Rather surprising for a twelve-year-old girl in 2003. She loved drawing and her favourite colour was purple. We called her Tash. Those were the only things I really knew about Tash. Until the last few months of her life.

Throughout the next two years of operations and exhausting and debilitating treatments, Tash remained a quiet, smiling presence at our family gatherings, but eventually, Doreen and Eddie were told that there was nothing else to be done.

During those last months of her life, their home became a regular meeting place for family and friends, brought together by their love for a child they'd watched grow into a teenager, and who were silently coming to terms with the fact there would be no more milestones to share with her, only memories. I was so proud to be part of this family who were sharing their grief and, in the process, healing themselves. For the first time, I really felt I belonged somewhere. My feelings of loneliness were nothing compared to the torment her parents and brothers must have gone through. I couldn't imagine what it must be like to lose a child, or a sister.

The middle child of three wonderful children, Tash was the only girl. It must have been so hard for Daniel and Conrad to watch their sister suffer, and share the pain and anguish of their parents as she slowly slipped away from them.

Finally, she was confined to bed, unable to do anything for herself, but always smiling, always happy to see her friends and family, and often staring at something on the wall of her bedroom. Months before she died, she told her parents not to worry about her because angels were waiting to take her to heaven. Could she see them there, watching over her? I wonder.

Natasha passed away peacefully during the night of 9th July 2004. Her funeral was attended by so many people, including other young cancer patients. It must have been a surprise for everyone to hear Elvis singing 'Return to Sender', but this was Tash's request, relayed to her parents when she was still able to communicate. What a mature young lady and how fitting.

After the service, everyone gathered outside and we were each given a balloon to send off into the sky. The colour? Purple of course. Tash's favourite. The first balloon took off on its own.

"That one's for Steven," someone cried.

Steven was living in London at the time and, naturally, disappointed that he couldn't be there to say a final goodbye. So, later in the evening I called him to recount the events of the day.

"… and one of the balloons flew away on its own, so that one was for you," I told him. There was silence at the other end of the phone.

"Steven, are you OK?"

"Mum," he said, "what colour were the balloons?"

"Purple," I replied. "Why?"

"A purple balloon just flew past my office window."

Unbelievable. But true. Not a blue, yellow, red or green balloon, but purple, a fairly unusual colour for a balloon. And Tash's favourite.

What I learned about Natasha during those last few months of her life was that she was a very brave and caring young lady who loved her family and her friends around her. I believe the balloon was her way of saying, 'Bye, Steven, I haven't forgotten you and I know that you're thinking of me.'

Natasha on her First Communion Day

32

A Family Reunion

England, 2009

Olwyn turned sixty on 21st April 2009 and I was determined to be there to celebrate the occasion. We'd talked on the phone about having a reunion with other members of our extended family, so Clive and I were expecting an eventful three-week holiday.

Our three weeks passed very quickly, the highlights being Olwyn's birthday and the reunion. Invitations were sent to everyone on both sides of our family and everyone responded. It was amazing.

The party started at three in the afternoon and finished about midnight. We thought there might be too many people but, the way it worked out, all Dad's side of the family came early in the afternoon and all Mam's side arrived about six, just as the others were leaving. It was great to meet cousins I hadn't seen since I was a teenager. And there were two I'd never met at all.

Some families live in the same country or even the same town and rarely see each other. My Dad and some members of his family were estranged for many years, so it was great to meet all of our cousins and to rebuild the bridges which had been torn down by some long-forgotten quarrel. Although it wasn't possible to have long conversations with everyone, it was an amazing reunion.

Whenever I visit England, I always need to return to my hometown of Bishop Auckland. This is where I was born, where I went to primary school and grammar school and where I worked as a teenager. I love to stroll down Newgate Street, walking in the shoes of my childhood.

In my teens, I would march up this street to the cenotaph with the Girl Guides each November, walk home from school to save the bus fare or meet my friends on Rossi's corner. This is the street of my youth, the road to everywhere and it hasn't really changed much. With one major exception: when I take a walk down Durham Chare, just off Newgate Street, I smile. It reminds me of the song *Big Yellow Taxi* – 'they paved paradise and put up a parking lot'. That's what they did to our small terrace of three houses. It's now a car park and I wonder how it was possible for three families to live in such a tiny space.

On my walk down memory lane this time, I was browsing the aisles of WH Smith when I noticed a book about the history of Bishop Auckland. Olwyn had sent me a copy a couple of years before because on page 115 was a photo taken of my class at St Anne's Primary School in 1950. I was standing at the back without a name. The word "unknown" in its place. She'd written to the authors so they could update their information, so I was keen to see the photo with my name on it. But that didn't happen. I eagerly picked up the book and found the photograph. I wasn't even there. My photo had been removed completely. Like I didn't exist. Very strange. And another reminder that I didn't belong here.

One of my best memories of that trip home was the birthday lunch I shared with Olwyn and Carol. I couldn't remember the last time we'd all been together like that, just the three of us. I left home when Carol was twelve and Olwyn eighteen, so there was never time to form adult relationships with either of my sisters and spending two or three weeks between their homes with their families around was not conducive to sharing feelings, memories and experiences.

No, I'm sure the three of us had never had a sisterly get-together. Something to remember the next time I visited.

However, I do have cherished memories of times spent with Olwyn when she was living in Evesham, after separating from her husband, Tim. This was a very hard time for her, and I'm grateful that I could be there to share her thoughts and feelings and reminisce a little about our childhood.

During those cosy evenings, I learned how my leaving had affected this sister of mine, who had been my responsibility throughout primary and into grammar school. It was I who had waited impatiently for her to get ready each morning, and it was I who took her home. Being five years younger, she had looked up to me until she was about fifteen. Then she seemed to want everything I had.

When I left home, there was an enormous gap in the lives of all my family, but I left Olwyn with the problems I was running away from. She was now the eldest and so took on more responsibilities in the Golf Club when I left, then at the Kings Head where our parents moved to a few months later. At twelve years old Carol was much too young to be a barmaid in the evenings or a waitress on weekends.

Living away from home without my family, I thought it was easier for those left behind. They might miss me, but they wouldn't be homesick and depressed; they'd get on with their lives and move on without me. I was the only one who was suffering. Now, I realise that there's always an empty space in their lives too. There's always someone absent at their family gatherings. And it's not just the physical absence.

They say you never miss what you never had. That's not strictly true. I still miss the close relationships with my sisters that I might have had, and that they never had with me. But somehow we've managed to preserve and nurture the seeds which were planted within us during those early years. A fridge magnet Carol's husband,

Alan, gave to each of us says it all: 'Sisters by chance, friends by choice'.

33

I Still Remember You

England 2015

She loved butterflies and poppies and sunflowers. She was my little sister. Carol. It doesn't make sense. This is not supposed to happen.

Carol was born on 29th September 1954. My sister Olwyn was five-years-old and I was ten. She was our baby sister and we loved and cared for her. She was a beautiful mistake Mam would say. And she was. She was beautiful, but never a mistake.

When Olwyn came over to Australia in July 2015, she was concerned about our sister's health. Carol was having a lot of pain in one of her legs and had bought an automatic car as she was finding it difficult to drive. I spoke to her on the phone and told her I would be there when she needed me. She said she was OK but I booked a flight for 11th October anyway.

By the time Olwyn returned to the UK, things had taken a turn for the worse and Carol was unable to leave her bed. But she didn't want me to change my plans. She was sure things would improve and she wanted to be better when I came. But a text from her daughter Charlotte a few days later delivered a different message: *Come now. I think Mam's hanging on for you.*

During a visit to the hospital for a checkup, Carol had been diagnosed with breast cancer. Within a day of being diagnosed, she had chemotherapy and shortly after was admitted to an end of life hospice. It wasn't breast cancer. She was in the advanced stages of lung cancer. She was dying! How did this happen so quickly? It was now essential that I get there as quickly as possible.

Julianne decided to accompany me and we managed to book flights to travel within two days, Business Class, courtesy of my ever thoughtful and generous son.

"You need to be fully alert when you get there," he said, so we were able to sleep and arrive refreshed. The company of my daughter distracted me from my thoughts of Carol and helped me to enjoy the comfort and care provided by the possession of a Business Class ticket. I was truly grateful for my son's thoughtfulness.

We arrived in Newcastle on Sunday 28th September and went straight from the airport to the hospice. Carol looked so ill and it was difficult to hold back the tears as I smiled and placed a kiss on her cheek, hugging her to me to hide my distress. Doctors had said she could leave us at any time. But she was so strong. "Don't be sad," she said. "It is what it is."

Next day, the 29th was Carol's 61st birthday and we all knew there wasn't much hope of another.

But as the days wore on, she rallied. She was out of bed and into a wheelchair in front of the French windows in her room. When I arrived she still had her beautiful hair. Then it started to fall out, handfuls at a time. Of the three of us, Carol had the best hair and she wore it to her shoulders. She was so proud of her hair, and it brought tears to my eyes to see her smiling and saying it was only hair.

Olwyn brought some headscarves and we each had fun trying them on and taking photos. We talked about our youth and reminisced about our parents. Much to our joy and amazement, Carol seemed to be getting better, and by the time I had to leave England, plans were underway to take her home. She was adamant that she was going home. My plan was to return in December, so although our goodbyes were very emotional, I left thinking I would see her again. But I never did. She died on 24th October, one week after I left, and it broke my heart that I was unable to be there for her funeral.

I returned to the UK in December 2016 to spend Christmas with Olwyn and to share memories of Carol, our little sister we would never see again.

34

Moving On

Perth, 2018

Sadness is exhausting, and there were times in my life when I was perpetually tired. Those times of sadness are very rare now, but there are moments which come out of nowhere, when I'm once more overwhelmed by the intensity of a yearning for the once-familiar places and people. When I hear friends talk about their families, when we get together with Clive's family, I still feel the emptiness, but not as much, just for a short time and not for now, but for the past, for something I can never retrieve. But my parents are always here in my heart and my head – Dad in the songs he used to sing and Mam in songs and snatches of the phrases and advice I still live by.

They say that though two people may travel together, they never make the same journey, there are always different memories. It's true, and that's one of the great things about reminiscing with family. There are no shared memories of my childhood in Australia. But there are many years of memories to share with our children, our grandchildren, and my extended family. And more to come.

I've been living away from my family for most of my married life – fifty years in December 2018. I've shared more special occasions with Clive's family than I have with my own. In fact, they know me better in some ways. But they don't know the person I used to be.

As much as I've lost, I've also gained. I'm very grateful to have been so totally accepted by my adopted family, though they must have found it difficult at times to understand my moods. They migrated to Australia, but they were together. I've shared the pain and joy of their family but never my own. The births, birthdays and weddings of my nieces and nephews, the funerals of my sister-in-law, mother-in-law and our beautiful niece Natasha. But I was absent from my sisters', cousins' and friends' weddings and the funerals of my parents, grandmother, aunts, cousins and, more recently, my beautiful sister Carol.

I'm happy with the choices I made. Life is what you make it. The path I chose has brought lessons and challenges to overcome, and because of them, I've become stronger and wiser.

But I didn't make this journey alone. My husband and children travelled with me. Clive bore the brunt of my bouts of depression, anger, grief, and self-pity, never really understanding the reasons for my sudden outbursts. Most importantly, he gave me the confidence to be whatever I wanted to be. He survived two heart attacks. The first, one evening in 1992, when he was about to drive to Midland Technical College, where he lectured in the Real Estate Salespersons' Course. I had to bully him into letting me take him to Armadale Hospital, from where he was quickly transferred to Royal Perth. The following day he underwent surgery to insert a stent.

In 1998, when his second heart attack occurred, he was alone in the house, painting our lounge ceiling. Luckily he recognised the signs, called an ambulance and phoned Ivan, his brother-in-law, who lived close by. Another trip to Armadale, another transfer to Royal Perth and another stent insertion.

And, of course, our children, who must have wondered why their mother would often excuse herself from family gatherings when they knew she wasn't sick. My beautiful daughter, always a chatterbox since the night she was born, is my best friend and always there when I need to talk, with her no-nonsense approach to problems. My handsome and clever son, the quiet one, is such a good listener when I need advice and help with more practical problems. I'm so proud of them both, as individuals and for what they have achieved so far in their lives. They are the first generation of our family in Australia and I want them, and their children, to know where they came from and how their father and mother got here. It was a rough passage at times, but we have emerged relatively unscathed.

Some clever person once said that there is always a cost to even the most willing of self-exiles. And they were right. But yes, I'm home now. And have been longer than I realised.

About the Author

Born in the North East of England, Val now lives in Perth, Western Australia with her husband, Clive. She taught English as a Second Language for many years, most recently in the Australian Migrant English Programme at Central TAFE, until her retirement a few years ago.

Val is now a volunteer with the ReadWriteNow programme, helping to improve the literacy of adults.

www.ingramcontent.com/pod-product-compliance
Lightning Source LLC
Chambersburg PA
CBHW071226080526
44587CB00013BA/1514